Scientific Laws of LEADERSHIP

Scientific Laws of LEADERSHIP

Achieving Success and Reaching Goals

Kalyan Sagar Nippani

Viva Books

New Delhi | Mumbai | Chennai | Kolkata | Bengaluru | Hyderabad | Kochi | Guwahati

Publisher's note

The views and opinions expressed in this book are the author's own, and do not necessarily reflect the opinions subscribed to by the publisher.

Every possible effort has been made to ensure that the information contained in this book is accurate at the time of going to press, and the publisher and author cannot accept responsibility for any errors or omissions, however caused. No responsibility for loss or damage occasioned to any person acting, or refraining from action, as a result of the material in this publication can be accepted by the editor, the publisher or the author.

Every effort has been made to trace the owners of copyright material used in this book. The author and the publisher will be grateful for any omission brought to their notice for acknowledgement in the future editions of the book.

First Published 2014

Viva Books Private Limited

- 4737/23, Ansari Road, Daryaganj, New Delhi 110 002
  Tel. 011-42242200, 23258325, 23283121, Email: vivadelhi@vivagroupindia.net
- 76, Service Industries, Shirvane, Sector 1, Nerul, Navi Mumbai 400 706
  Tel. 022-27721273, 27721274, Email: vivamumbai@vivagroupindia.net
- Megh Tower, Old No. 307, New No. 165, Poonamallee High Road, Maduravoyal, Chennai 600 095
  Tel. 044-23780991, 23780992, Email: vivachennai@vivagroupindia.net
- B-103, Jindal Towers, 21/1A/3 Darga Road, Kolkata 700 017
  Tel. 033-22816713, Email: vivakolkata@vivagroupindia.net
- 7, GF, Sovereign Park Aptts., 56-58, K. R. Road, Basavanagudi, Bengaluru 560 004
  Tel. 080-26607409, Email: vivabangalore@vivagroupindia.net
- 101-102, Moghal Marc Apartments, 3-4-637 to 641, Narayanguda, Hyderabad 500 029
  Tel. 040-27564481, Email: vivahyderabad@vivagroupindia.net
- First Floor, Beevi Towers, SRM Road, Kaloor, Kochi 682 018
  Tel. 0484-2403055, 2403056, Email: vivakochi@vivagroupindia.net
- 232, GNB Road, Beside UCO Bank, Silpukhuri, Guwahati 781 003
  Tel. 0361-2666386, Email: vivaguwahati@vivagroupindia.net

www.vivagroupindia.com

ISBN: 978-81-309-2487-8

Published by Vinod Vasishtha for Viva Books Private Limited, 4737/23 Ansari Road, Daryaganj, New Delhi 110 002.

Printed and bound by Raj Press, R-3, Inderpuri, New Delhi 110 012.

SUB-00026

To

My Twins Bubbu and Bubbi

(But for whose relentless invasion of my computer

I could have finished this book much earlier.)

Honey and Nina

Mummy and Daddy

and

All those giants upon whose shoulders I humbly stand in an attempt to see further...

Contents

'The fact that modern physics, the manifestation of an extreme specialization of the rational mind, is now making contact with mysticism, the essence of religion and manifestation of an extreme specialization of the intuitive mind, shows very beautifully the unity and complementary nature of the rational and intuitive modes of consciousness; of the yang and the yin.'

— *Fritjof Capra, author of* The Tao of Physics

Acknowledgements

I WOULD BE FAILING IN MY DUTY IF I DO NOT MENTION Stafford Beer, the founder of Management Cybernetics in making me think on these lines. I also thank Dr E.G. Rajan, Founder and Chairman, Pentagram Research Center (Cybernetics and Informatics) for being a catalyst in my humble attempt to demystify management cybernetics, thus making it applicable to everyday life.

Listen Ye, to what by nature will be told
And to your mind and heart forever dearly hold
Everyday a new journey you begin
Remember the laws and you shall always win...

Prologue

'THE WHOLE OF SCIENCE IS NOTHING MORE THAN A refinement of everyday thinking,' said Albert Einstein. Taking this statement to its logical conclusion one can say that scientific thinking and the scientific method, when refined and adapted appropriately, can be applied to understand, and conduct oneself in, everyday life. Thus, the laws, axioms, principles and postulates of science can be employed for everyday excellence in personal and professional life.

In anticipation that this idea may sound a little outlandish to some, let me in all fairness delve a little deeper into its foundations. 'Science' is derived from the Latin word *scientia*, meaning 'knowledge'. It refers to any systematic knowledge or practice that is aimed to increase human understanding of how the world works.

In the Webster's Dictionary science is defined as 'systematized knowledge derived from observation, study, and experimentation carried on in order to determine the nature or principles of what is being studied'. What is implied by this definition is the idea that conclusions are made on the basis of empirical evidence (i.e. evidence that comes from experimentation and observation).

The scientific method refers to all the techniques employed for studying phenomena for acquiring knowledge. It can also be for correcting and upgrading previous knowledge. In general, the techniques of the scientific method comprises:

(a) observation
(b) measurement
(c) experimentation
(d) replication
(e) hypothesis formulation and testing

Empirical observation, experimentation and objectivity are acknowledged to be the foundations of science. Scientific theories and laws are formed based on the scientific method. The scientific method incorporates all the principles and procedures for systematic and objective pursuit of knowledge about the natural phenomena.

Thus, a true 'scientist' is someone who studies the world around him objectively using the scientific method and thereby draws conclusions that are true and correct. Reality is understood and acted upon as it really is. Actions based on truth and correctness bring intended results. Thus, application of the laws and principles of science in everyday life would ultimately result in everyday success. Laws of science apply to leadership in a different context too. Leadership skills are cognitive skills that neuroscientists have located in specific regions of the brain, predominantly in the frontal lobes. These include, among others, working memory, task initiation, defining and achieving goals, prioritization, emotional control and focus. Thus, it's all just simple science end to end for success in personal and professional life.

Deduction and induction are the two main logical thought processes employed by science. In deduction particular conclusions are arrived at from a general premise. An example is presented below:

1. All men are mortal.
2. Socrates is a man.
3. Therefore, Socrates is mortal.

In induction, generally conclusions are arrived at based on existence and observation of particular instances. An example of this is as follows:

1. Crows at Chennai are black.
2. Crows at Delhi, Kolkata and Mumbai are black.
3. Therefore, all crows are black.

I have used both induction and deduction while elucidating and applying the laws of science for everyday leadership. This is because while some laws 'denote' and very precisely define reality, others 'connote' and indicate possible definitions. Even to laws that denote, there are many related connotations. This is precisely what makes science an interpretative, creative and evolving realm of human endeavour. Unless seen relationally, laws make no sense in themselves. At its core, like any other realm of intellectual endeavour, science is an 'interpretative' understanding of the world. 'It would be possible to describe everything scientifically,' said Einstein himself, 'but it would be without meaning, as if you describe a Beethoven symphony as a variation of wave patterns.'

Scientific laws and postulates capture the essence of phenomena in a nutshell. A scientific law is a comprehensive statement of fact intended to explain an action or a set of actions. It is sometimes expressed as a numeric equation. A scientific law is a descriptive generalization about how certain things occur in the natural world under specific conditions and circumstances. It serves as a comprehensive summary of hitherto non-related facts. Laws of science are formulated by following scientific method and logical reasoning. Most of the scientific laws are simple statements and accepted as universally true.

The gigantic edifice of science and all its branches are founded on laws and postulates. A scientific theory is more similar to a law than a hypothesis. A theory, however, is more elaborate and complex while a scientific law is generally concise. A scientific theory is a detailed explanation of the natural world, which incorporates facts, laws, axioms, theorems and hypotheses.

An axiom or a postulate is a statement that is considered self-evident although not always actually proved or demonstrated. It is a truth that is accepted as such and serves as evidence to other truths. It is therefore a starting point from which other facts are logically derived. Unlike theorems, axioms are not derived by the principle of deduction or demonstration.

Science provides for flexibility and open-ended evaluation in its pursuit of knowledge and truth. That is why we have a 'hypothesis' and 'axioms'. A scientific hypothesis is nothing but conjecture based on observations or logical reasoning. It can be proved to be true or falsified by evidence. A hypothesis is a statement that is amenable to testing and can serve as a foundation to build further theories and explanations.

When an observation is confirmed repeatedly by unbiased and objective observation it becomes a scientific fact. There is a creative dialogue and a dynamic symbiosis between the pursuit of science and that of other intellectual endeavours. While the famous thinker Robert K. Merton established the socio-cultural roots of scientific advances, Auguste Comte proved that social sciences, of which leadership is a part, makes use of scientific methods such as observation, experimentation, empirical investigation and replication. Durkheim, the father of modern rationalism, regarded social life as made of 'social facts'. Social facts are objective 'things' that extend to each individual in the society. Max Weber provided a more interactively scientific method to understand social phenomenon by his idea of 'Versthen' – interpretative analysis of human behaviour. This book attempts to take these ideas to their logical conclusion. Laws of science would be applied scientifically to everyday life in all its dimensions with special emphasis on leadership.

In the past, many have wondered if something as non-material and intangible as the human mind can be subjected to objective scientific analysis. Today all such doubts have been set to rest with advances in clinical psychology and neuroscience. What is more, from the perspective of social 'science' even attitudes can be measured. Attitudes are enduring patterns of beliefs which influence the behaviour of individuals. Scaling techniques such as the Thurston and Lickert scales are used to quantify attitudes.

All human emotions are nothing but chemical reactions. Neurotransmitters that flow between nerve cells are the cause of human emotions. Anxiety, irritableness, depression, etc. are as much the cause of chemical imbalances in the brain cells as tranquility, enthusiasm and elation are due to chemical balance. Today, we know which neurotransmitters produce which emotions and also the neurotransmitter's sub-systems. Serotonin deficiency, for instance, causes depression. We also know that there are over 18 sub-types of serotonin receptors.

With all due respects to the romantics at heart (I am an incurable one myself), today science is finding evidence to what was earlier considered 'love' by poets and writers of the idealistic genre. Love is nothing but an offspring of chemicals called pheromones. Pheromones are chemicals that trigger many types of natural behaviour. Many animals and even plants communicate with each other through pheromones. So, even the most subtle of human sense and sensibilities are within the ambit of scientific study and interpretation. Laws of science therefore can be used to understand daily life.

Way back in school I was an avid watcher of Carl Sagan's stupendously popular television series *Cosmos: A Personal Voyage*. The distinguished American Astronomer ends one episode by declaring that modern science has a thorough knowledge of the human body. The human body is made up of 35 litres of water, 20 kilograms of carbon, 4 litres of ammonia, a kilogram of lime, 800 grams of phosphorous, 250 grams of salt, a few grams of flouring, iron, silicon and 15 other trace elements. He then walks to a large cauldron, pours these very chemicals into it and stirs the mixture. 'Where is life?' He asks poignantly. Carl Sagan is merely pointing to the immense twilight zone where science of matter and the science of the spirit that matters blend seamlessly. In this book, each scientific law is followed by 'evidence' of its application in everyday personal and professional leadership. While doing so, I will be frequently drifting in and out of the twilight zone.

Modern science is now making forays into the womb from where it in fact originated. Civilization relegated that pristine science into the realm of religion and the occult. Now civilized modern man is scientifically reevaluating what was systematically shunned. The present book is not about the converging trend between science and spirituality. But, this fact has to be made explicit to the reader since the book frequently dips into the borderline area where the science of matter and that of the human spirit meet.

In his book *The Tao of Physics* Fritjof Capra, the renowned physicist, explains how he underwent an intensely spiritual experience that revealed to him the unity between science and ancient religious mysticism. He explores deep into the borderline area between the world of science and that of the spirit in his book. Among other things, he establishes that ancient spiritual and philosophic thought of the east had already known what modern science is today in the process of discovering. Thus, in the explanation of the laws of science in their practical application to everyday life, it is only natural that I at times take recourse to spirituality and philosophy for purely pragmatic reasons.

Life is indeed a rally and a race. One must have both speed and endurance to win in every endeavour that one undertakes. However, more often than not we end up running without purpose or direction. Worse still, we also run frantically for the wrong purpose and in the wrong direction. Can the laws of science open up stunningly new vistas whereby you can win spectacularly by running for the right purpose and in the right direction? And incredible as it may sound, can you at times win without running? Do read on and find out, the laws of science never lie...

Notwithstanding the title, and at the risk of getting into an intricate debate, I must confess that leadership is both a science and an art. There is ample academic and empirical proof that the divide between the two, both in theory and in practice, is very thin. It is at times, semipermeable. The evidence for this is in this very book too where each 'scientific' law and concept is substantiated by examples of leaders who 'artistically' enacted them.

1

Setting a Lifetime Purpose and Leading by It

KEPLER'S FIRST LAW

The orbit of each planet is an ellipse which has the Sun as its focus.
The planets move in different orbits and at different speeds, yet the Sun is always their focus and point of reference.

KEPLER'S SECOND LAW

Each planet moves in such a way that the (imaginary) line joining it to the Sun sweeps out equal areas in equal time.
The line from the Sun to any planet describes equal areas in equal times.

AS A CELESTIAL BODY GOES AROUND ITS FOCUS – THE Sun – have the purpose of your life, your lifetime purpose, as the focus around which you shall nurture your thoughts and actions. You may not always be at the same level of proximity with it, and may at times, have to stray away or consciously move away. Your movement around your ultimate reference point in life may thus not be a perfect circle but an ellipse. But it does not matter. Your 'orbit', the path you tread in life, will be centred on your lifetime purpose. Thus all shall be well in your heart and in your mind and therefore in all that you do in life. Thus will you yourself become the brilliant Sun, the force and focus to which people will be drawn and around which they will revolve.

Leadership is based on two fundamental sources – positional authority and charisma. The former is based on one's location in the power hierarchy. The latter has its wellspring in the personal character, conduct and vision of a leader. The twain may overlap. Yet what has a lasting impact and inspires the willing loyalty and trust of others is intensely personal. It is not a matter of an office order or a memo.

The greatest of leaders in human history are the ones who have found their lifetime purpose and lived through it and up to it. This book is full of examples of such leaders. It is not that great leaders find their lifetime purpose. It is because ordinary people find their lifetime purpose that they become great leaders.

Barry Diller had an illustrious career of nearly 40 years in the entertainment industry. He oversaw many milestones in films and television while working for ABC, Paramount and Twentieth Century Fox. On being called a visionary, he responded 'The first time they said it, I thought they were talking about eye charts. I don't see anything full-blown. I never have. I see what interests me'. Diller was passionate about an idea, about what he believed in. This propelled him to actualize it spectacularly throughout his life.

When you find your lofty lifetime purpose and strive towards it sincerely, your teammates shall gradually make it their own too. You thus begin to lead effortlessly, as evident in Kepler's Second Law.

When thus you move along in life you shall always stay in tune with your ultimate purpose. Your teammates will always be within your line of sight and vice-versa. There will be an invisible bond that attracts and binds them to you. When you are the focus of others, they too shall stay connected to you at all places and at all times. Physical proximity does not play a determining role here.

Your aura will inspire them. Seneca, the famous thinker, said, 'As in sprint and chariot contests, keep to the "inner track" in the race course of your life.' The world bombards us with experiences, pleasant and pleasurable, unpleasant and unworthy.

The self that is like a white sheet of paper when you are born is increasingly scribbled upon by myriad experiences as you grow. You cannot stop the scribbling nor wipe it all clear. What you can however do is evaluate every experience with self-approved standards of judgement that is engraved in the inner self. And how can you do that if you do not keep close to your inner track?

Finding a lifetime purpose is one thing. Conducting daily life in rhythm with it is quite another. Finding the rhythm is quite simple. Just keep your purpose, vision and mission in life close to you, invisible to the others and under your cloak if you have to, yet always close.

Trivialities that appear larger than life and wayward temptations of immediate yet illegitimate gains will always attempt to throw you off-track. Yet, remain faithful to the values that are dear to you and the lifetime purpose which you cherish and believe in. All influences that tend to divert you shall then wither away of their own accord.

When you remain thus centred and steadfast even as you surge ahead on your chosen path, others shall be attracted to you and shall follow you effortlessly, as if it were a natural course, like rivulets pouring down the hills from all directions joining the mighty river.

LAWS OF MOTION

A body in one dimensional motion always moves only in one plane and in a straight line. Two and three dimensional motion includes – magnitude and direction.

Magnitude

It is the amount of quantity present. Physical quantities which are fully and completely specified by only their magnitude are known as scalars. An example of magnitude is speed.

Direction

A quantity has a direction which defines it. These quantities cannot be defined just by magnitude. A complete knowledge and definition of them requires one to specify their direction also.

LET VIRTUE SET YOUR LIFE IN MOTION, WITH THE good, the right and the just as the grids that provide the dimension to your existence. Move on the straight path of truth whatever be the dimensions and you shall find joyful glory in the end and along the way too. In the midst of the world out there let your movement be on different directions in different lines of thought and action. Thus, you shall be moving at times through tumultuous situations yet are ever on an unobstructed track both within and without. Thus you shall be as a boat is in the eye of a storm, tossing amid waves yet with its sail set and in movement towards its port.

Another aspect of magnitude is quantitative in nature. You need 'magnitude' in life, for magnitude is quantity. Numbers and the tangibles are indeed essential – money, material objects, success and mutually beneficial relationship. These bring comfort, fame and joy, which are some of the intangible results that subsist within magnitude's qualitative form. Even this being so, have direction to a destination for it is the essence of both life and livelihood.

There are many who have all the material possessions in copious quantity and yet are desolate, dejected, depressed and lonely. They possess things that can be quantified in life but not those that are qualitatively subtle. They lord over the tangibles and yet are lost to the intangibles. They have things and objects but lose the sense of direction in which to carry them.

With time, these very cherished objects will turn into a heavy weight and the bearer of them will turn into a beast of burden. Quantitative achievements are all mere signposts and banners. They proclaim loftily what you have gained yet cannot reclaim what you may have lost in the process. As a wise man once said, 'We live in an age that is all signposts and no direction'. Be therefore in constant movement in life with a dimension that must be diligently chosen and in a direction where intervening gains or losses would turn to mere incidentals.

Above all, you must have the inner propensity of movement and strength to progress ahead in spite of obstacles and setbacks. A leader above anyone else must have faith in himself. The faith, if formidable enough, can have the potency to rewrite fate. While fate is born out of despair, faith is both of the mind and the heart. It can heal a soul affected by fatalism. Faith is an offspring of belief and as it grows it becomes the latter's mentor. Faith turns more profound. It turns deeper than belief. It permeates reason and understanding.

The story of Christopher Paul Gardner is a sterling example of 'faith' in oneself overcoming 'fate'. His story has inspired the movie *The Pursuit of Happyness* with Will Smith playing the lead role of Gardner. Gardner was born in the midst of poverty, hunger and illiteracy. This continued to plague his adult life too. Abandoned by his wife, he took up small-time jobs and lived in shelters for the homeless with his little son. Once the father-son duo had to spend their night in a bathroom of Bay Area Railway Station. Destiny seemed to have abandoned him, but faith in himself kept him going.

One day while making some sales calls Gardner met with Bob Bridges, a stockbroker in a red Ferrari and befriended him. He would one day drive his son in such a Ferrari, he promised himself, and enrolled for a fast track training programme. Although he came from an illiterate background and had no corporate connections or a college degree, he had faith in himself. He also joined as a trainee in Dean Witter Reynolds, a stockbroking firm. He was persistent in making calls to prospective clients and followed through each of them to achieve spectacular success. In 1992 he passed the licensing examination in the very first attempt and became a full-time employee of Dean Witter Reynolds.

Paul Gardner later on went to establish his own immensely successful stockbroking firm. Gardner never forgot his past. He has given back to the society what in fact the society had long deprived him. He has contributed millions of dollars to sponsor the projects of low-income housing and shelters for the homeless.

But this cannot happen on its own accord. For this to happen you need a measure of self-propelling momentum, as shall be seen in the following page.

Anybody who has been seriously engaged in scientific work of any kind realizes that over the entrance to the gates of the temple of science are written the words: 'Ye must have faith'.

— Maxwell Planck, Physicist & Nobel laureate

THE LAW OF MOMENTUM

Momentum is the quantity of force in a body. A heavy body moving fast is difficult to stop. A smaller or lighter body moving at a slower speed is easier to restrain. Conversely, a smaller body, say a bullet, moving at great speed rips through anything that is in its way.

WE ALL MOVE ALONG IN LIFE PROPELLED BY THE inexorable and inescapable hand of time. Some sail along gracefully with a smiling face, some trudge reluctantly while still others drift. Do not resist the ethereal flow of life through time by creating boulders and barricades in its way. Even if you are adrift, remember, rough seas make tough sailors. For this is how skilful sailors are made. And this is precisely how men and women of steel are tempered. If you can control the sails of the boat of your own life, the winds and storms will not matter much. Do not dwell your mind and heart on petty intervening incidentals. Focus instead on consequent fundamentals.

Disproportionate and exaggerated fixation with inconsequent incidents, which are like debris rubbing against the hull of a ship, have only one result. They will only turn the music of the waves into a cacophony of noises.

In life let your momentum be guided by the nature of circumstances. When you are confident and in control of the means to an end and when rivals are few or powerless, move along at a placid and steady pace. Look around and pick up a few flowers and fruits along the path. When relatively powerless and enemies are many, let your momentum be swift and be endowed with ruthless precision. In either case, let your momentum in life be reinforced by magnitude of all that is lofty and be guided in the self-chosen direction.

PRINCIPLE OF IMPULSE

Impulse is a spontaneous impelling force;
an impetus.
It is a sudden change in the momentum of a body caused over a very short time. Impulse equals the change in momentum produced by the force in this time interval.

OBSERVE AND EXAMINE LIKE A SCIENTIST EVERY SUDDEN emotion or urge that prompts a spontaneous act. Thus you will not be impulsive and commit errors in thought, word or deed. When you understand and control your impulses, you will segregate them from your instinct. Impulse is yin. Impulse is also yang. Impulse is good and desirable. Impulse also is bad and avoidable. It is a coin with two sides like many things in life, defined by the self, the circumstances, and the self in different circumstances.

Your momentum in life is often deeply affected by impulses – occasional, sporadic or regular. Impulses have their source both external and internal to the self, and their locus is either in the heart or the mind.

Be aware and vigilant of the externally generated impulses. At times, they have the power to produce a distorted impression of reality and truth in you. You thus think the impulse is of your own will and volition while the truth is quite otherwise. Be also vigilant of internally generated impulses. At times, they lead you to destruction by turning you blind to the warnings of their external counter-parts. Pay heed therefore to every impulse of the mind and heart. Then you shall wisely discern that which you impulsively find pleasurable, yet by refined instinct understand that it is not preferable. You will therefore also know the difference between that which is pleasurable yet fleeting, and that which is preferable and enduring.

POWER PRINCIPLE

Power is the rate at which work is performed or energy is transmitted.
It is the amount of energy required or expended for a given unit of time.
Power is the rate of change of work done or the energy of a sub-system.

'EVEN THIS SHALL PASS AWAY' THE BUDDHA IS BELIEVED to have said at his deathbed. Nothing can stop the inexorable march of time nor resist its dialectical creative–destructive powers. Even action or work that is lofty, noble and laudable is within the bounds and confines of time. What you need is the power to execute the assigned and self-assigned tasks in time. With your mind being clear, right and high, by your conscience being cleansed of all that is contrary to your conviction, you will have in abundance the energy that transforms work to effective action. Your actions will thus produce the change you intend to see in yourself and burn up all the intervening hurdles that you may contend with in this process. The power you possess would be the average and the optimal amount needed to be expended for the result intended. It will be moderated as the occasion demands. Thus, it shall grow cumulatively.

Garner, therefore, the power within and without, for power is but energy in action. Just as the singular arch of rainbow is constituted by many colours, all arising out of colourless light, the power you possess is but energy that is at once physical, mental, emotional and spiritual. Its possessor transforms and is likewise transformed. Power is self-nurturing, for it grows with its right use. It is likewise self-destructive, for it rebounds to destroy if misused. Power is tangible only in its active, non-dormant form, while energy can be 'potential' or stored up unused. Align therefore your energy with power. What then are the different forms of energy? You will know when you flip this page to the next one.

LAWS OF REFLECTION AND REFRACTION

The Law of Reflection

Light is known to behave in a very predictable manner. If a ray of light could be observed approaching and reflecting off of a flat mirror, then the behaviour of the light as it reflects would follow a predictable law known as the law of reflection.

Law of Refraction

The refractive index of a transparent substance is measured when light enters the substance from a vacuum. The greater the value of the refractive index, the greater the bending of the light. Refraction is caused by the fact that light travels at different speeds in different media.

The Law of Mirror Types in Optics

Concave mirror is a converging mirror and a convex mirror is a diverging mirror. Concave mirrors form both real and virtual images while a convex mirror always forms a diminished virtual image.

LIGHT ENERGY IS THE ENERGY THAT ILLUMINATES AND shows the way ahead. It dispels ignorance. Its conjunction with science is a contradiction in terms like say, 'bright–darkness' or 'square–circle' which exist in words only and not in factual reality. Reflection is a vital component of leadership.

In fact, there is a direct relationship between enlightened leadership and higher levels of reflective capability. The higher the reflective power, the higher the degree of 'enlightenment' in leadership. Like a bright beam of light, the illuminating energy of the leader very lucidly and predictably reflects his or her vision and purpose and that of the organization too.

You must reflect the core values and vision of your organization in each of your overt word and deed. You are the mirror upon which the face of the organization is visible to all its stakeholders. The stakeholders include employees, customers, vendors, investors and the general public.

To be a good leader you must have refractive power too. This is at once both a diverging and correlative power. As a captain of a ship does when an undetected iceberg is looming large straight ahead there will be at times a need to deflect the course of events and the direction in which the team or organization is moving. You must not only reflect the values and vision of the organization but do so in an appropriate and desired manner. The perception of something by others is at times more important than what the thing is in itself. By the power of refraction, the leader at times plays a corrective role and also presents the organization as it ought to be seen by the stakeholders.

Jack Welch, the former CEO of GE, was indeed called a 'Neutron Jack' for his drastic downsizing. Welch became Chief Executive Officer of GE in 1981. In just a matter of two years, i.e. in 1983, he launched a full-throttled 'fix, sell or close' strategy. He revalued every business that GE was into. If there was a problem or if the business was not making profits, the strategy was to either sort out the problem quickly or sell it off to the highest bidder. The final option was to bury it with a sigh of relief, writing it off as sunk cost. This resulted in massive closures and layoffs. GE shed over 80,000 employees. Jack Welch was nicknamed 'Neutron Jack' because the people disappear but the buildings are left standing, just as a neutron bomb would decimate human beings but leave the buildings intact.

Yet he also made innovative changes in the area of human resource development at GE. He modernized GE and made it into a diversified conglomerate. He successfully implemented the Six Sigma quality programme throughout the organization. In 1980, when Welch took over as its CEO, GE had revenues of around $26.8 billion. When he left in the year 2000, the figure was $130 billion. GE was among the best corporations in the world. Rockefeller Jr., Louis Gerstner and Carlos Ghosn did the same with Standard Oil, IBM and Nissan as will be seen in this book later.

In a normal situation, what impinges upon the organization from outside, i.e. the incoming 'incident', and what is 'reflected' out is thus the same. The angles and images visible in both are the same. At the individual level, the leader must be both a reflective and a refractive thinker. Refractive thinking is self-referent and divergent in nature. It moves away from the known and explores the not-yet-known.

Reflective thinking is convergent thinking. It moves from the out there to the within. It begins from questioning or probing into the unknown and converges within the self. Thus, what is found out there is purged, crystallized and reflected by the self within. A critical mind is a convergent one while a creative mind is divergent in nature.

God does not play dice.

— Einstein

CRITICAL THINKING INVOLVES LINEAR LOGIC. IT IS unidirectional while being analytical like maths. Creative thinking on the other hand is not linear. It can flutter like a butterfly in any direction and land on a flower and savour its nectar. While the former depends on causality and attempts to pinpoint one precise solution to a problem, the latter gives different solutions to the same problem, if not at times redefining the problem itself.

A leader must strive to balance both. For, extremes of either will lead to cynicism at one end or unfounded fantasies and unreasonable wishful thinking at the other.

Einstein, stop telling God what to do!

— Niels Bohr

NEWTON'S THIRD LAW

For every action there is an equal and opposite reaction.

THIS LAW HAS TIMELESS ROOTS IN HUMAN ETHOS. IT IS known by many names in many cultures, one of it being Karma. Every action has a consequence or an effect that matches it in a most natural, logical, simple and equally inexplicable way.

Act in ways therefore, knowing well that the effects of the same shall return unto you, in equal proportion. The good thus begets good that returns to you. For it has been said by the seers of yore 'as you sow, so shall you reap'. If you have no belief in what the seers have said, at least do pay heed to Newton, the father of modern science.

Examples of the inexorable operation of these laws are abundant in human history. Perhaps, history itself is in a way an enactment of this simple and ethereal law. As a literary convention, I cite a few.

Even great and powerful emperors could not escape the inevitable results of cause–effect, at times called the principle of Karma in the Indian socio-cultural lore. Good acts ultimately beget you good and vice-versa. At a time in human history when Rome was the most powerful empire on earth and the Roman emperor was elevated to the status of a demigod, the law of action and reaction worked with clinical and ruthless precision. Powerful Roman emperors fell victim to their own greed, avarice, pride and deceit. Commodus was brutally murdered by his own army. Pertinax was executed. Caligula, Macrinus and Maximus are among other emperors who met a similar fate.

Adolf Hitler shot himself in his underground bunker. His own people summarily executed Mussolini and his body was hung upside down at a petrol station in Milan. As it is said, power has the propensity of corrupting the hearts and minds of people. Absolute power has the potential to do so absolutely. Bernard Ebbers was at one time among the world's most powerful CEOs and the company he co-founded was regarded as one of the best among global corporations. Bernard Ebbers was born into the family of a travelling salesman. While hopping between colleges, he worked as a milkman and bouncer. Ebbers began his business by operating a chain of motels in Mississippi. In 1983 he joined a group of like-minded investors in the newly formed Long Distance Discount Services, Inc. (LDDS). By the dint of his business acumen, he quickly rose to become its Chief Executive in 1985. The company acquired over 60 other independent telecommunications firms, changing its name to WorldCom in 1995. The same year he entered the Mississippi Business Hall of Fame.

In 1997, he made the startling announcement that WorldCom was making an unsolicited bid for MCI Communications. The acquisition was successfully completed in 1998 and won him fame and glory. He figured among the 25 most powerful people in networking by Network World 1999, and found listing in the TIME Digital 50 the very same year. Success if not taken in its stride and if not tempered with humility and ethics breeds hubris. What follows is the inevitable entropy and decline.

Stupendous success led to hubris, conceit and greed. A scandal broke out and in 2005 he was convicted of fraud. Presently he is serving a 25-year prison term in Louisiana.

Ego and actions that germinate out of it led astray even acknowledged leaders. Henry Ford II had an uneasy relationship with Lee Iacocca, a brilliant manager who worked his way up from a Junior Engineer to become the President of Ford Motor Company. The meteoric rise and popularity of Iacocca made Henry Ford II, the Chairman, restless and insecure. Iacocca developed many automobiles for Ford, including the incredibly successful Ford Mustang. Yet, Henry Ford's prejudice reigned supreme. Iacocca was unceremoniously shown the door. Chrysler Corporation lapped him up. At Chrysler Iacocca unleashed his magic and turned it around from near closure to a formidable rival of Ford Motor Company. Massive inroads were made into Ford's market share. Under Iacocca's stewardship Chrysler came out with the Dodge Aires and Plymouth automobiles. They were affordable and economical on fuel – just what America needed during the oil crisis. Then came the Minivan which is arguably among the top in minivan sales in the USA even today. Henry Fords II's action had boomeranged on him.

If I have seen further,
it is only by standing upon the shoulders of giants

— Sir Issac Newton

HEISENBERG'S UNCERTAINTY PRINCIPLE

Attempting to measure accurately the position of an elementary particle leads to uncertainty in measuring the particle's momentum accurately.

There is the inevitable uncertainty in the ability of an observer to measure more than one quantum variable accurately at a time.

Quantum entities display both wave and particle nature depending on the observer's frame of mind.

POSITION AND VELOCITY CANNOT BE MEASURED AT THE same time. If you want to moonwalk in life with a velocity of your leisure and liking, be sure you are in a position that allows you to do so. It doesn't matter if it's higher or lower – the 'positioning' matters. There is an intimate connection between wave and particle natures of quantum objects. Likewise, an individual displays an 'either-or' nature based on your own view and attitude. You actually determine the other person's response towards yourself. Much as we all want order and predictability, we live in a world that is perpetually uncertain. The first step towards certainty is to objectively accept uncertainty.

The movement of matter, say a planet, is more predictable in time and space than its smaller counterpart, say a sub-atomic particle. In life too, it is often the smaller everyday events that turn contrary to expectations with wider and much larger ramifications. A tiny and apparently trivial aberration has in its womb a major upheaval. Take not therefore the apparent trivialities for granted. Tackle each uncertainty one at a time. For, it is more probable that when you begin in doubt you may arrive at certainty. Certainty at the outset will gradually sink you in the quicksand of doubt.

The Tatas were not very much in the forefront of India's business world until the 1860s. It was Jamsetji Tata who made an audacious decision to break with the past and venture into the manufacturing industry. Until then Tata had only trading interests. The first industry which the Tatas entered into was textiles. Jamsetji's innovative mind and visionary acumen in a situation of uncertainty can be seen from the fact that he introduced ring spindle when the devise had not yet been put into full commercial use even in the USA, where in fact it had been invented.

His audacious adventures in the realm of uncertainty went beyond technology and made forays into the field of management. He experimented with hitherto unknown managerial systems, wherein he himself became salaried Managing Director, reporting to conventional Board of Directors. This was much before the term 'Corporate Governance' had emerged even as an idea.

Jamsetji Tata's tryst with uncertainty went against convention and generally accepted ideas of colleagues, friends and competitors. This lent the spectacular aura of originality to his thought process. Just as he had plunged into textile industry, he made forays into steel and hydroelectric power generation in India. According to the prevailing wisdom, the then existing laws of the colonial government, level of technology and the huge money that was required to go into these segments made people pronounce that they were foolish decisions. These odds seemed to only strengthen the will and resolve of Jamsetji Tata. He worked towards achieving his ends obsessed with not just business success but with the idea of nation building through infrastructure development. He walked the untrodden paths and made way for others to follow with his uncanny ability of embracing situations of uncertainty.

Acknowledge the colourful bouquet of uncertainty around you, for then it shall carry you to the altar of seamless certainty.

2

Leadership through Interpersonal Excellence

THE PHYSICAL AND CHEMICAL LAWS OF MATTER

Anything that occupies space and has mass is known as matter. Matter exists in three states: (1) solid (2) liquid (3) gas.

Solids have definite shape and volume. Liquids have definite volume but take the shape of the container.

Gases have neither a definite shape or a definite volume. They take the shape of the container and fill it completely.

Even within each, there is a difference in their kind according to their 'inner' nature. Solids are of different sub-types:

crystalline (with regular bonding), molecular (with weak bonding), and ionic (held by ions of opposite charge).

Liquids are either compressible (can be compressed), viscous (relatively less free flowing), steady (not very free flowing), laminar (tending to flow turbulently) gases are ideal (hypothetical), natural and noble (chemically unstable).

SOLIDS, LIQUIDS AND GASES ARE SIMILAR TO STATES OF the subjective *mind* and states of existence at a personal level. When the emotive content is incorporated into the state of mind it becomes a state of being. At the inwardly looking personal level, it is by introspection that one discovers one's mind-state and by empathy the state of being. When the reverse happens, i.e. by 'extrospection' (If you don't find that word in the dictionary please consider it coined), the mind and states of being others are recognized. For inner clarity and outer harmony such an exchange between the inner and the outer is essential. The mind-state is a reflection of the state of being and vice-versa. Both determine and are in turn determined by each other. Both ultimately are dynamic energies that make up one's overall personality. Hence, when the term 'mind-state' is mentioned in this book, it refers to 'state of being' also.

A leader above everyone else must understand these energies and thus apply that knowledge in conducting himself or herself in personal and professional life. To indicate how, if not exhaustively, I regress back in time to about 3000 years to a unique branch of science called Ayurveda.

The ancient science of Ayurveda classifies such dynamic energies into three types – *vata, pitta,* and *kapha.* This is not a rigid typology of kinds of people but a 'here and now' view of the dominant energy within a particular person as externally apparent in his or her dynamic personality trait(s).

Vata, pitta, and *kapha* are only personality 'traits' and not personality types. They are in conjunction with dynamic energies or *gunas – sattva, rajas* and *tamas.* Thus the violent, conniving and vindictive individual, if he were *vata, pitta* or *kapha* with *tamo guna* can become loving, righteous and benevolent if his or her *guna* changes to that of *sattva.* Even those endowed with *sattva guna* tend to at times swing from one extreme to the other with time and circumstances. Yet, when *sattva guna* is imbibed deep into the mindset and state of being, these swing to the abyss, are but temporarily.

Take for instance, J.D. Rockefeller, the American industrialist who revolutionized the petroleum industry and was the richest man on earth for many years. With inflation taken into account and the value of the dollar, Rockefeller would be more than thrice as rich as the Bill Gates of today. As money flowed in, the good and kind Rockefeller somehow slipped into the gunas of *rajas* and *tamas.* His son Rockefeller Jr seemed to be on the aggressive *rajas* mode. Both father and son handled a strike of 9000 workers of Standard Oil poorly. The National Guard was summoned by them to deal with the workers sternly. That they well did and led to the infamous Ludlow massacre where 24 workers perished. The image and reputation of the Rockefellers was at its nadir. Standard Oil and Rockefeller were portrayed as betrayers of the nation. Added to this, anti-trust suits were filed in Court. Pictures of a large octopus (Rockefeller and Standard Oil) with its tentacles around a ship (the country) splashed across America.

Tamas and *rajas* at their worst then turned to *sattva* at its best. The Rockefellers went through rigorous introspection, as all leaders must after a stupendous failure. Rockefeller Jr went on record to state that the Ludlow incident was the most important thing that happened to the Rockefeller family. Both father and son found their innate *sattvic* leadership qualities again. All-out efforts were made at a total image and credibility rehaul. The rest is history, as evident in just a few of the many things to their credit. The charitable trust called Rockefeller Foundation, the founding of the University of Chicago and Rockefeller University and a long list of lofty contributions to humanity through them.

This is what Ron Chernow, biographer of Rockefeller, had to say: 'What makes him problematic – and why he continues to inspire ambivalent reactions – is that his good side was every bit as good as his bad side was bad'. Well, one thing is indisputable about Rockefeller the leader of sorts. In the dialectical struggle between the *tamas–rajas* combine and *sattva*, the latter triumphed within him ultimately. That's what matters.

A brief mention of Bill Gates here would not be out of place. Gates too began right earnest to become the world's richest man from being a college dropout. On Microsoft's way to superstardom, he had to often consciously snuff out rivals, sometimes in a ruthless mercenary manner. A slew of anti-trust suits followed. The *sattva*-turned-*rajas* nature met its nemesis. At one point during the anti-trust trial, he looked utterly forlorn, dejected and red-eyed. He is said to have broken down and wept in his office later.

Perhaps that is the inexplicable way how *sattva* gains ground – from the womb of *rajas* and *tamas*. After handing over the reins of Microsoft to his long-term friend and college Paul Allen, Bill Gates along with his wife fully immersed himself in philanthropic work. The global impact the Bill and Melinda Gates Foundation is already making is already more than the efforts of many governments put together.

Just as Rockefeller is today remembered more for his impact on humanity through philanthropy, perhaps Bill Gates too will be. I for one would value the eradication of a single disease in one country more than a Windows Vista in every PC in the world. After corporate leadership, Gates is displaying community leadership.

Therefore, a trait or set of traits is not permanent or immutable, but amenable to change. The traits are value-neutral and objective entities. Yet, subjective and qualitative elements of being enable them to change. All matter is energy and energy can change from one form to another. If so why can't we – as individuals and as a collectivity – change for the better? Each state of being has free will. It has an inherent freedom of choice.

The mind-states are of three broad categories. In a solid mind-state there is compactness and rigidity of attitudes and beliefs. Change within is slow and change from outside is resisted. This is the *kapha* personality. The liquid state displays more flexibility and amenability. It is able to accommodate change and is receptive to external influences. This is the *pitta* personality type. The gaseous state displays very less compactness and stability of attitudes and beliefs. It is extremely flexible and nebulous.

I reiterate, that I pass no value judgements on the preferability of one mind-state or the other. It will soon be demonstrated that the appropriateness of each is highly situation dependent.

Solids are of three subtypes depending on the type of bonding – crystalline, molecular and ionic.

The first type bonds regularly and normally. Molecular solids display a weak bonding. Ionic bonds are characterized by coming together of opposites. Liquids likewise reveal qualitative differences within themselves. The same goes for gases too. These are characteristic of qualitative differences in the intrinsic states of mind of all types of dynamic energies. This subtle differentiator is akin to the *gunas* or dynamic qualities mentioned earlier.

The hybrid of the mind-being states and the *guna–dosha* attributes is presented in the table that follows, which will give a simple snapshot view of the matrix. It will be amply clear from this that neither a particular mind-being state nor a particular *dosha* state is good or bad *in itself*. Each in itself can be pitiably pathetic and avoidable or sublimely supreme and desirable. What makes the difference is the qualitative *guna*.

A few practical examples as evidence will be appropriate here to substantiate what may appear to some as a little too pedagogic. It will also serve to dispel any doubts regarding the veracity of the matrix. The 'state of being' refers to all the qualities constituting someone who exists. It is the 'essence' or worth of an individual in qualitative terms and net-worth of an individual in quantitative terms. The state of being includes within its ambit the mindset of an individual or a group and reflects their essential nature or personality.

Just as individuals have a 'personality' so do organizations. Strange? Not really. 3M has the personality of being innovative and Johnson & Johnson that of being conservative. Reliance is aggressive while Tata is cautious (with the exception of locating the Nano Project in Singur perhaps) and socially committed. Southwest Airlines is employee friendly while Infosys is ethical. Here is the catch – as is the leader who steers the organization, so is the organization itself. The leader's persona is reflected in that of the organization and permeates through it. William McKnight joined 3M as an assistant bookkeeper and went on to become President and then the Chairman of the company from 1949 to 1966. He embodied the spirit of adventure of ideas of 3M's founders who failed in their initial ventures but quickly found ways of turning failure to success. McKnight made the management of 3M delegate responsibility and encourage men and women to exercise their initiative. His fundamental leadership style fostered a corporate culture that is a fertile breeding ground for individual initiative. Innovation can be best summed up in his own words:

> 'As our business grows, it becomes increasingly necessary to delegate responsibility and to encourage men and women to exercise their initiative. This requires considerable tolerance. Those men and

> women, to whom we delegate authority and responsibility, if they are good people, are going to want to do their jobs in their own way.'
>
> 'Mistakes will be made. But they will not be as serious in the long run as the blunder a leader could make by snuffing out creativity in his team. The management will make a mistake if it undertakes to tell those in authority exactly how they must do their jobs. Management that is destructively critical when mistakes are made kills initiative. And it is essential that we have many people with initiative if we are to continue to grow.'

In the field of medical care, one has to be cautious and conservative. The cause of humanity is far greater than making quick bucks at the cost of quality. This was the philosophy of Robert Wood Johnson and his two brothers, who founded Johnson and Johnson. This attitude characterizes the company even to this day.

Reliance is characterized by a go-getter do or die approach. The entrepreneurial spirit of its founder Dhirubhai Ambani continues to be the life breath of Reliance. The group still runs with Dhirubhai's expectation of 'beating deadlines and not just meeting them'. Another quote attributed to him sums it all up 'I am deaf to the word no' he had said. The cautious approach and corporate social responsibility of the Tata group is but an offshoot of the personality and lifetime purpose of J.R.D. Tata and his successor Ratan Tata.

During his tenure as CEO of Southwest Airlines, Herb Kelleher's colourful and cheerful personality spawned a unique corporate culture that endures even to this day. Southwest employees are known to take themselves lightly – often joking and interspersing flight announcements with popular songs – but taking their job quite seriously. Southwest stood afloat in the midst of many turbulences that hit the airline industry in the US and was many times among the top five Most Admired Corporations in *Fortune* magazine's annual polls. Fortune also called him perhaps the best CEO in America.

Infosys personifies Narayana Murthy's principles of ethical conduct in his own personal and professional life. Its founder and present mentor set high standards of ethical conduct for himself that have by and large become the ethos of Infosys. He firmly believed that ethics and moral values transcend legal framework.'As society evolves, what is in the realm of ethics and values moves into legality', he said. In other words even if 'legal' strictures do not as such prohibit a business transaction, Narayana Murthy would not do it if it did not have the ethical legitimacy. Such a value system, he said, was the true strength of Infosys.

Matter Type	*Guna Type*		
Dosha Type	*Sattva*	*Rajas*	*Tamas*
Solids	Crystalline	Molecular	Ionic
Kapha	Serenity Compassion Wisdom	Greed Gluttony Selfishness	Chaos Instability Neurosis
Liquids	Compressible Viscous and Steady flow	Unsteady and Turbulent flow	Incompressible Inviscid Erratic
Pitta	Correct cognition Empathy Right perception	Lust for power Aggressiveness	Wrath Vengeance
Gases	Ideal	Noble	Natural
Vata	Brilliance Creativity Poise	Fear Anxiety Tension	Lack of clarity Uncertainty

SECOND LAW OF THERMODYNAMICS

Entropy of an isolated system that is not in equilibrium will tend to increase over time.

THIRD LAW OF THERMODYNAMICS

As a system approaches absolute zero temperature, all processes cease and entropy of the system approaches minimum value.

UNIVERSAL LAW OF INCREASING ENTROPY

Over time, differences in temperature, pressure and density tend to even out in a physical system that is isolated from the outside world. Entropy is a measure of how far this evening-out process has progressed.
The larger the system, the more applicable is this law.

THE BUDDHA CALLED IT *ANITYAVADA*, THE DOCTRINE of impermanence. Everything that exists perishes. Material science calls it entropy. Entropy is the inevitable disintegration of things – yet at different speeds. When you are not in equilibrium within yourself and also with the significant others (family, friends, colleagues for instance) you tend to get isolated. With isolation, the pace of entropy increases.

Remember this – you may be aloof, but you are seldom alone. You may be solitary while the loneliness in it is of your own making.

You are an individual 'in' the system. You have your distinctive individuality, but it is born out of togetherness at different levels with people out there. Making yourself too aloof, be it by pride or low self-esteem, will lead to quicker and irreversible entropy within you and your team.

The changes in the socio-psychological environment is to the soul what physical exercise is to the body. There is growth and progress when you are part of the multi-faceted life out there. Isolating yourself from others will be the beginning of personal and professional entropy. The famous General Benedict Arnold who fought on the American side during the Civil War isolated himself from his colleagues. He felt neglected and joined the British side. He lost his reputation and fortune.

Orville H. Gibson was the creative genius who founded the famous musical instruments company Gibson. He came up with new designs of the guitar and mandolin. The phenomenal demand for his products made him partner with four investors. But all did not go well. Gibson began to quarrel with his partners. Even trivial issues such as who gets to stand where in official photographs were blown out of proportion. Eventually, he went to a self-imposed exile and sold his stock in the company.

Louis-Joseph Chevrolet was the co-founder of the Chevrolet Motor Car Company. He was a mechanical genius and a popular racing driver. All was going well until Louis Chevrolet walked over the thin line dividing individuality and egotism. He developed differences with his partner Will Durant over the design of a new car. He was antagonistic to all ideas that were not in line with those of his own. Entropy caught on. He sold his shares in the company to Durant and faded into oblivion. Will Durant in turn did not learn from the failure of his former partner. He achieved fame and fortune as the founder of General Motors, yet he too fell victim to personal entropy that affected his professional life.

He was on the tip of the wave of the so-called 'Roaring Twenties' that saw business and stock market boom. It was a time of wealth and excess and of course the dangers of speculation, which many conveniently ignored. The abundant optimism and surging bull market came to an abrupt halt on what is now infamously known as the 'Black Tuesday'. This was the Great Crash of 1929 when the stock markets of the US nosedived as never before.

Durant, like other financial giants including the Rockefellers, bought large quantities of stocks in order to demonstrate to the public his confidence in the stock market. This was against the advice of all his well-wishers. The slide could not be stopped. By 1936 he was bankrupt. Durant was seventy five years old. He and his wife lived on a little pension he received from General Motors. Later, a stroke left him a semi-invalid. He ended up managing a small bowling alley in Flint, Michigan, until his death in 1947.

You will, as a consequence of the debilitating power of entropy, be reduced to nothing. Your place in the value chain of your personal and professional life will be a big zero if you are so lucky to be a spectacular failure. If not, it will be a moderate and insignificant zero that will not raise even an eyebrow.

Be therefore a part of the world while retaining your distinctiveness. The world will then respond to you and only add to your uniqueness.

William Durant, the founder of General Motors ended up managing a small bowling alley in Flint, Michigan. Benedict Arnold carried his individualistic attitude even after the civil war and failed in his business ventures. Orville Gibson was diagnosed mentally instable and eventually died a loner. The legendary Louis Chevrolet died near penniless.

Be less curious about people
and
more curious about ideas

— Madame Curie

THE JOSEPHSON EFFECT

The effect associated with the tunneling of electron pairs across an insulating barrier separating two superconductors.
It refers to the passage of paired electrons through a weak connection between superconductors.
A current of paired electrons (super current), will flow in addition to the usual current that results from the tunneling of single electrons.
When two superconducting materials are separated by a thin insulating material, electrons can travel from one to the other producing a super charge even in the absence of voltage difference between the two materials.

WHATEVER BE YOUR STATION OR CALLING IN LIFE, YOU must and can display leadership. One of the roles of the leader is akin to a good conductor of energy in science. When two individuals at high and equal levels of importance interact, it must be only to enhance the effectiveness, success and happiness of those who depend on both of them. These two leaders are 'super conductors'. It is the responsibility of the superconductors to together churn out a super charge from otherwise ordinary and unenthusiastic individuals.

The 'dyad' or two-person interrelationship between superconductors can be that of husband-wife, business partners, heads of two inter-related departments, heads of state, etc. The superconductors can also be more than two in number.

The energy transmitted by the two or more superconductors will be more than their individual energies and will increase cumulatively as it traverses through the organization. Even if a few are influenced by this, it spreads like a current to the others who may be different in many ways. For, real enthusiasm and happiness are contagious. They beget their likes in others.

The energy of the leader must pass through others like a current charging and enthusing them. As Ralph Waldo Emerson said, 'Enthusiasm is the mother of effort, and without it nothing great was ever achieved.'

One of the best ways to enthuse people is to communicate with them appropriately. Words of hope and courage can be powerful instruments to reach out to the mind-being states of people and alter them. A few examples of this include the ever-resounding 'I have a dream' speech of Martin Luther King in 1963 in which he hoped that one day his children would 'live in a nation where they will not be judged by the colour of their skin but by the content of their character.'

Yet another example was when Winston Churchill addressed his countrymen when Natzi Germany was at its aggressive best. He ignited the spirit of hope and enthusiasm of his nation when he declared 'We shall go on to the end... we will fight on the seas and oceans, we shall fight with growing confidence and growing strength in the air, we shall defend our island whatever the cost may be, ... we shall fight on the beaches, we shall fight in the fields and in the streets; we shall fight in the hills; we shall never surrender'... A leader is truly a 'dealer in hope'.

The Commencement address of Steve Jobs at Stanford University in the year 2005 is another gem in this context. In this speech Steve Jobs talks of his days at college. He would sleep on the floor of his friends' room and collect empty coke bottles from the campus and return them for the 5 cents deposit to buy food. He recollects having walked nearly seven miles every Sunday to a Hare Krishna temple for the free meal offered by the temple. The experience was far from romantic, but Steve Jobs says he loved it. In spite of all this Steve Jobs followed his heart and intuition, and went on to establish Apple Computers and Pixar Animation Studios.

Steve Jobs ends his speech with the following words 'Stay hungry. Stay foolish'. This speech inspired so many young people across the world. In fact, there is a recent IIM CIIE publication titled *Stay hungry. Stay foolish.*

Words spoken by the leader must result in inspiring action. Examples to this are famous 'Blood and Iron' speech of Otto von Bismarck, the Prussian statesman who brought over the unification of Germany in the early 1870s. Other examples include Subhash Chandra Bose, who declared, 'Give me toil, tears and blood and I will give you freedom' and Patrick Henry, a prominent figure in the American Revolution, who said 'Give me liberty or give me death.'

Leaders invigorate others not by just words but by deeds. Who can be a better example to this than Mahatma Gandhi, who lived out his *Ahimsa* and *Satyagraha* concepts in all their dimensions. 'Be the change you want to see in the world', he said. And he for one really did. Leaders are verily 'greater' than anything that can happen to them.

As a child of God,
I am greater than anything
that can happen to me.

— Dr A.P.J. Abdul Kalam

GAUSS THEOREM (THE DIVERGENCE THEOREM)

A vector is any directed variable quantity that can be broken into components. There is a relationship between the outward flow of a vector field on a surface to the behaviour of the vector inside the surface.

PERSONAL AND PROFESSIONAL LEADERSHIP CONSISTS in taking charge of your inner thoughts and your inner energy. Only then can the leader direct others and things out there. The world out there and its dynamic situations and events are variables that are either already 'quantified' or are susceptible to quantification. Quantification is the tangible evidence of quality.

The amount of money in your bank, the number of vacations you take with your family, the time you spend with your near and dear and of course with just yourself, etc. are numerical indicators to the sublime concepts of love, power prosperity and peace. The visible expression of you and your leadership qualities will in turn have the effect of reinforcing the invisible qualitative repository of the same.

Understand the nature of each variable as it is visible and also its nature that is beneath its surface and is not easily visible. Understand too the overt and outward flow of behaviour of people and the unseen attitudes beneath the surface. Grasp the intentions beneath actions of others as also the components that make up such intentions. Go to their roots and see what waters and nurtures them. You will then understand the actions at the visible plane and the intentions that play beneath the visible.

AVAGADRO'S HYPOTHESIS ON GASES

Equal volumes of gases at the same temperature and pressure contain the same number of molecules regardless of their chemical nature and physical composition.

PEOPLE IN THE 'GASEOUS' STATE OF MIND, THOUGH different in every other respect, tend to possess similar attitudes which affects their behaviour. They may be from different social strata, from different cultures and often playing different roles. Yet, under conditions that are standardized for long, their differences in knowledge and skill set levels get evened out. This was first revealed in the historic Hawthorne studies. Certain path-breaking experiments on human behaviour were carried out by George Elton Mayo at the Hawthorne Works of General Electric Company in Chicago between 1924 and 1927. The results of the experiments made a huge contribution to organizational development in terms of human relations and motivation theory.

It was established that work is not a simple, individual human activity. Even when a particular task is assigned to an individual and is performed individually, it is an intensely group-oriented and group-directed activity where there is an interplay of attitudes and beliefs at both formal and informal levels. An individual is consciously and unconsciously subjected to social demands of the group. Many socio-psychological controls determine the attitudes and guide actions of individuals.

He indeed is a true leader who understands this and manipulates the conditions that influence performance to get the best out of both the team and the individual.

GRAHAM'S LAW OF DIFFUSION OR EFFUSION

Under similar conditions of temperature and pressure, the rates of diffusion of gases are inversely proportional to the square roots of their densities.

GASES – DALTON'S LAW OF PARTIAL PRESSURES

When a number of gases are present in the form of a mixture in a container, then, the total pressure exerted by all gases is equal to the sum of the partial pressures of various gases in the container.

WHEN DIFFERENT PEOPLE IN THE GASEOUS STATE OF mind are present together in a situation where there is a shared task, the total pressure exerted by the situation and the task on them is equal to their partial pressures. The leader above all else must recognize this. If not, the minds thus influenced individually and collectively will in turn act upon the leader as a combined and unwelcome pressure on him or her.

Mark Antony faced precisely such a situation. When Julius Caesar was brutally done to death by certain conspirators, chaos reigned high in Rome. None could be trusted, for, there were so many factions among the ruling echelons. His own commanders were confused and the citizens of Rome were blinded by rage. Their minds were volatile. In spite of the immense pressure he faced, Mark Antony was in a state of equanimity and mental equilibrium. He was thus able to deploy his innate oratory skills and presence of mind skilfully to swing the public opinion to his favour.

It may appear that the gaseous mindset is too chaotic to be easily amenable to control. But the truth is quite the contrary. Such a state of 'individual mind' or 'group mind' is easily susceptible to control and manipulation. Gay Lussac's law discussed on page 59 precisely sums this up.

JOULE–KELVIN EFFECT

When a gas under pressure is allowed to move through a small orifice to a region of low pressure, it experiences a fall in temperature. The change of temperature with pressure is called Joule-Kelvin effect.

YOU MUST KNOW WHICH MINDS IN GASEOUS STATE TO put under the pressure and turn the heat on and which not to. You must also know for how long. Some agitated minds need to be relaxed selectively. A good leader finds or devises an 'orifice' or opening through which that agitated mind can pass on placidly to a situation where the pressure is lower. In other words, you must at times take the heat off some highly volatile minds. Otherwise, that singular agitated mind has the potential to destroy itself and disrupt the other minds in its proximity. Therefore, while you turn the heat and pressure on, you must also skilfully and selectively provide relief and leisure. The leader must act as a soothing balm at times and instil confidence and a sense of security and well-being in the team. Even as Ms Ranjana Kumar implemented her path-breaking restructuring measures in reviving the Indian Bank, she went about meeting the unions regularly and making them an integral party to her decisions. She took steps to address their insecurities and assuaged their fears of closure and retrenchment. She made them change their defeatist attitudes and give their Bank their best.

At the depth of the Great Depression in the US, William Carrier found his air-conditioning firm Carrier on the docks. At a time when lay-offs were routine and a precondition to getting bank loans, Carrier refused to send home even a single employee. This reassured and greatly comforted employees at all levels in the company. With fears at rest and the pressure off, they were at their best in their jobs helping Carrier survive the Depression and became one of the leaders in air-conditioning and heating systems.

PASCAL'S LAW

*The pressure exerted at any place
in a fluid in a
closed vessel is transmitted undiminished
throughout the fluid.*

WHEN THE TEAM IS IN A FLUID MIND STATE, THERE may be pressure on the leader who takes on the role of a 'container' or the vessel which holds them. The leader only needs to apply his or her pressure or authority on one or a few selective minds and the effect would be transmitted and experienced by the entire set that comprises all the fluid-state minds. As this happens, the message of the leader does not diminish but only grows exponentially.

GE under Jack Welch became an organization in the liquid state taking the shape of the 'container' or the unique socio-cultural and political concomitants in which its divisions and subsidiaries operated. Jack Welch not only restructured the way business is done at GE, but also laid down what businesses to do and what not to.

His formula was for GE to be either No. 1 or 2 in any business sector. If the forecasts predict otherwise, Welch would not go near it. If already in it, while not in the top two positions, he would simply pull out. This at times led to large scale lay-offs and closures. Within the first few years of taking over as CEO of GE, between 1981 and 1985, he cut around 1000,000 jobs. He was likened to a neutron bomb that vaporizes people but leaves buildings standing intact. (This is not time or place to delve into the rationale and ethics of what Welch did).

PHOTOELECTRIC EFFECT

A phenomenon in which negatively charged electrons are emitted out or negated from solids, particularly metals, when exposed to (electromagnetic) radiation of certain wavelengths.

THE LEADER HAS THE ABILITY TO IMPACT PEOPLE IN THE solid-state mindset characterized by rigidity of thought in general and the rigidity that may don the attire of negativity. This negativity includes negative thoughts, attitudes and deeds. A good leader negates negativity. It's a double negation purging process. To achieve this you must fine tune your own thoughts to a particular wavelength to impinge on that of those in the solid-state mindset. You thus make them introspect and reform their thoughts, words and deeds. By reforming and purging their thoughts you further reform and purge those of yourself too. You are therefore, reformed and purged. This reformation is visible and tangible, more often sooner than later as qualitative performance and quantitative achievements in life.

The amenability of a mind in the solid-state to new ideas is rather low and slow. So, as a strategic act, the leader's wavelength must be different when such minds are approached as distinct from those of the liquid and gaseous mindsets. By precisely planning every thought, word and deed and with the practised patience of a scientist you can like an exorcist cast out the most virulent of negative traits even in a personality that possesses an apparently incorrigible solid-state mindset. The same ideas and emotions need to be conveyed in different wavelengths or frequencies to the three mindset states – the solid, the liquid and the gaseous. As is the mindset, so are the attitudes. As are the attitudes, so are actions. And as are actions, so are the results.

GAY-LUSSAC'S LAW OF COMBINING VOLUMES

Two substances which combine in a gaseous state always react in rational and simple volume. When allowed to do so, gases naturally form compounds with each other in simple definite proportions.

THE ADVANTAGE OF A TEAM FORMED WITH MINDS IN A 'gaseous' state lies in the fact that there is a natural blending of the 'mind-stuff' consisting of ideas, attitudes and beliefs. Minds in such a state often respond rather than react with each other. When they do react, it is rational and simple.

Thus the method to control such a group-mind is likewise rational and simple. Whatever is rational is in fact simple.

The leader is like a charioteer, so to say, in the midst of a race. There is one offbeat way to exemplify this, provided the reader has no qualms about the team being likened to horses. (In fact, many horses of pedigree are loved and cared for so much so that I often wish I was born as one of them.) Let me give the example as an allegory. In the epic blockbuster movie, *Ben Hur*, the protagonist by the same name is a rich and respected Jewish Prince who is betrayed by his childhood Roman friend Messala. He refuses to budge and snitch on some of his people who are building public opinion against subjugation of their country to Rome. He is offered power, glory and the friendship of the Roman emperor himself in exchange for switching his loyalty to Rome. He refuses.

Ben Hur becomes a slave because he does not want to be a puppet to Messala, who comes to Judea as a military commander. A strange twist of fate makes him the adopted son of a famous Roman General. Yet Ben Hur returns to Judea to search for his mother and sister. He meets an Arab Sheik with a magnificent stable of four majestic white

Arabian horses. The Sheik cares for and treats the horses like his own children.

His obsession is to make them win the famous Roman chariot race contest where the best in the world participate. Ben Hur, a fine charioteer himself, observes the practice sessions at the Sheik's camp. The horses, despite being the finest, are never able to complete a circle around the arena without a hitch. The Sheik blames the charioteer.

Ben Hur understands that though each horse is exceptionally the best individually, as a team they were a collective failure. This was because the unique and dominant quality of each horse was thus far being ignored. While Altair was mature and steady, the youngest Aldebarn was quick and restless. Antares and Rigel too had special individual traits. Ben Hur therefore suggests that the horses be rearranged in such a manner that each horse is able to express its individuality to the fullest. Thus, together they make a team that is more than the sum of its parts. He decides to enter the race when he hears that Messala is the reigning champion of Rome. Ben Hur trains the horses and builds a special bond *between* them and *with* them. Together they stunningly win the chariot race defeating the wicked Messala.

Today, every leader has the unenviable task of having to do a 'Ben Hur' every day. Well, it's all simple. Know your horses, understand them, bear empathy with them, nurture the individuality of each and rein them up together skilfully – and the race is as good as won.

3

Leadership Energy

TYPES AND PROPERTIES OF ENERGY

Kinetic energy of an object is the excess energy it possesses by virtue of its motion. Negative work of the same magnitude is required to put the body in a state of rest again.

Rest energy of a body is that energy which is dormant. The body is in a state of inertia. This energy can instantly change into either potential or kinetic energy.

Potential energy is the energy that is stored within a body. It is called potential because, it has the capacity to be converted into other forms of energy.

Thermal energy is often understood as energy associated with heat or temperature. In thermodynamics, it is internal energy present in a system or an entity that is in a state of thermodynamic equilibrium. However, it also refers to the spontaneous flow of energy from one object to another.

Electromagnetic energy is self-propagating and has both electric and magnetic properties.

Light energy needs no medium to travel. It has a dual nature. It exists as 'particle' and as 'wave'. Light travels in transverse manner, perpendicular to the direction in which it advances.

ENERGY REFERS TO A VARIETY OF FORCES USUALLY conceived as 'fields' or subtle forms. In both science and spirituality there is commonality in belief that everything in nature, including the human body of course, is a playground of different types of energy and energy fields. The human body and the human mind are capable of perceiving, preserving and propagating these energies in the form of aura fields, rays, vibrations and radiation. Energy is the universal life force.

Different cultural traditions call this variously as 'Prana', 'Qi, etc., a field of science called scientific Vitalism. Energy is both from the body and reason. It is the very subject matter of both science and spirituality insofar as the subject is the human being.

The ancient Chinese theory of acupuncture, which is accepted the world over as an established form of alternative medicine, is based on what is termed the Qi energy in the body that constantly circulates the body through pre-determined meridians.

Electromagnetic fields present in an organism is a scientific fact. Harold Saxton Burr, a renowned professor of anatomy at Yale, called it the 'L' field. This field consisted of measurable and tangible qualities. He used standard voltage measurement instruments to churn off irrefutable evidence for such a field. Kirlian photography, named after its inventor Semyon Kirlian, can actually photograph different auras emitted by the human body. It could capture a spectrum of energy fields generated by living entities.

'Elan vital' of Henri Bergson is the life force that could be harvested and even stored up in inanimate objects. He equated its flow to a 'current'. Rupert Shelarate called them the 'morphic fields'. These are patterns that govern the development of forms, structures and systems. Wilhelm Reich, a famous psychoanalyst called this omnipresent bio-energy 'Orgone'. He had many illustrious followers. In fact the famous American College of Orgonomy was founded to delve deeper into the research of Reich.

It is indeed possible for one to detect the aura and Qi and its nature. Saints and seers throughout history had the power to 'know' the feelings and 'read' the thoughts of others as if instinctively. At a rudimentary level all of us have it and have experienced it at one time or the other. We instantly seem to know the nature of a person or the mood of a colleague even before we use our normal senses to actually 'see' an angry face or 'hear' a pleasant news.

The seers of yore have practised this science to perfection. Many have done it to such a level that they can even detect the attitude and moods of a person a great distance away.

Today, science accepts the fact that 'radiation' from a living organism, which is an overt expression of feelings and thoughts, can in fact be detected. The awareness of the interplay of these radiations or auras makes a qualitatively radical paradigm shift in the personality of an individual. The unique power of controlling inner energy is both the cause and consequence of personal and professional leadership.

For then do the body radiations limited by the body truly inhere in it and yet are set free. Radiesthesia, a word that when broken into two means 'radiation' and 'perception by senses', is the ability of an individual to:

(a) perceive by the sense that is non-sensory
(b) make others perceive by their senses what is non-sensory

One is thus a 'centripetal' and the other a 'centrifugal' force. Both are necessary. The followers must be drawn and magnetically attracted to you. They must also move away from your shadow and make forays on their own creativity and initiative, while being 'connected' to you.

The discoveries of Luigi Galvani in the field of neurological science and that of Mesmer too dispelled all doubts about the interplay of physical and spiritual energies. The divide melted further with the discoveries of scientists such as Mesmer who equated energy with a form of magnetism that is evident both in the inanimate world and the animate life. This is the bio-energy inherent in all living beings and blossomed fully in the human self. Scientists like Harold-Saxton Burr did extensive studies on the electromagnetic fields of organisms.

Having once again attempted to touch upon the borderline area between science and spirituality, albeit for a highly pragmatic purpose, I now present the forms of energy that will transcent the heuristic divide between all that is science and all that is supposedly not. This will pave way for further explorations on the laws of *Leadership Energy* that follows.

Muladhara is the energy of our sensing capacity. Thought too is energy as much as tangible matter is.

Swaddhisthana is the energy inherent in our thinking power. As it is with matter and thought, so is it with emotions, and the energy propelling emotive force is called *manipura*. The capacity to will is unique to each individual and the power of will is born out of *anahata*.

The energy that incubates matter, thought and will is *vishuddha*, the energy of embodying.

That energy which is born out of ego yet transcends itself to the level of the self without ego is called *ajna*. This energy is the one that flows outward from the self to the others. It is the highway that links itself and other energies to the world out there.

Finally there is the most elusive of all energies – the *sahasara*, the repository of imagination and illumination. If forever receives the reinvigorating 'light' of truth and knowledge by travelling between contradictions and balancing them. While being highly individualized, it is also like *ajna*, for in its pure form it merges seamlessly with the people and things out there.

Muladhara is the potential energy stored within every individual. It is full of latent potentialities.

Swaddhisthana is the dormant or rest energy in any individual. The thinking power is activated yet does not become the energy in action. The energy in action is the energy that gives materiality and tangibility to the thought energy. It is *vishudda* energy, which is kinetic in nature. It brings in change and movement.

The gravity of your will power churns out the *anahata* energy. It seeks harmony and balance. It has the capacity to transform individual will to personal and collective achievement in life and livelihood.

Ajna seeks a thermodynamic equilibrium between the individual and the society. The 'society' ranges from the dyad of two individuals (husband-wife, boss-subordinate, child-parent, etc.) to the team of significant others and the organization at large. It can propagate itself in a polarity of apparently opposing fields. It can display properties of both the individual and collective nature just as light energy does.

A leader recognizes his *muladhara,* understands it as *swaddhisthana,* converts it into *vishudda.* He uses his *anahata* energy to achieve individual and collective transformation of employees. He employs the *ajna* to maintain and sustain individual and organizational equilibrium in the midst of conflict and turbulence.

EINSTEIN'S THEORY OF RELATIVITY
($E = MC^2$)

Energy is equal to mass and speed of light multiplied by itself.
Energy and matter convert into each other at the speed of light.

THIS DECEPTIVELY SIMPLE EQUATION ESTABLISHES HOW a small amount of matter can release a huge amount of energy. Energy is everywhere, without and within. Ancient Indian philosophers and scientists have said that matter is ultimately energy. A 'mere' 1000 years later, modern nuclear physics has 'proved' it. In the long-drawn debate on the superiority of mind and matter, science today concedes that the former may actually reign over the latter.

All matter is energy and all that ultimately matters is energy. This is true at the psycho-somatic level of the individual and at the organizational level too. In a biological context, catabolic energy is evident when cells break down and anabolic energy is released when cells augment and grow. This destructive-constructive energy dialectics permeate the mind and being of every individual too. From the individual it is transferred to the team and from the team to the organization. The leader with predominant anabolic energy has the ability to build and inspire. Those with catabolic energy tend to destroy and instil despair. Since energy by itself is value-neutral and has no friends or foes, its nature depends on its usage. You are thus the architect of your own energy type.

Albert Einstein himself sums this up in a nutshell when he said 'The release of atom power has changed everything except the way of thinking... the solution to the problem lies in the head of mankind.' He was referring to the use of the energy of an atom. I draw the same conclusion with regard to the energy within each individual.

LORENTZ FORCE

It is the force exerted on a charged particle in an electromagnetic field. The particle will experience a force due to electric field and magnetic field.

THE LEADER MUST FILL THE HEARTS AND MINDS OF HIS people with positive energy. As mentioned elsewhere in this book in greater detail, the leader must likewise negate negativity. When the individual is sufficiently charged up with the spirit of enthusiasm, he or she is ready and open to the vision and message of the leader.

As a leader, your personal magnetism results in a field of attraction. Two types of motivation are thus evident – the 'electric' that sears through the team charging and inspiring, and the 'magnetic' which aligns them to your core vision and mission.

Energy is expressed as charisma or magnetism in different ways. Each leader exudes it in a different ideational and emotive frame of reference. Spiritual sages of yore saw it as sagacity and compassion. With Herb Kelleher of Southwest Airlines it was his rapport with people and with Narayana Murthy (Infosys) it is corporate ethics and simplicity. With Jack Welch (GE) it was the spirit of winning and focused action and with Richard Branson (Virgin Group) it is boisterous enthusiasm and adventurism. Each had most of the leadership qualities discussed in different contexts in this book but one or the other would dominate and be their Dominant Energy Differentiator (DED).

The word charisma is derived from the Greek word that means 'gift' or 'divine favour'. Charisma refers to a rare trait or set of traits found in certain people. These individually or as a combination include extreme charm and a 'magnetic' quality of personality, persuasiveness, supreme confidence, powerful communication skills, outstanding analytical abilities, nobility of character bordering on the divine, etc. Charisma is the uncanny ability to influence people's thoughts, emotions and thereby their actions.

There is a point where I differ with the Greek implication of the term. The word implies that people are 'born' with charisma. There is enough evidence in theory and practice of leadership that charisma can be carefully cultivated and nurtured. It can be achieved and not just acquired at birth. It can be learned and taught. Charismatic leaders 'manage' their image consciously and meticulously.

The power of a leader is vested in the strength of the authority that legitimizes leadership. There are three sources of authority – the legal, the traditional (rooted in tradition) and the charismatic. Charismatic leadership is by far the most enduring. In fact, leadership based on legal mandate and tradition are further fortified and consolidated if such leaders have charisma.

Although each leader has his or her unique leadership trait, the common set of traits by and large include:

(a) vision that ignites passion among others
(b) skilful and forceful articulation of the vision, i.e. communication skills
(c) sensitivity to the environment
(d) empathy to the ideas, feelings and needs of others
(e) willingness to make personal sacrifices and an overt display of the same
(f) unconventional behaviour that enthuses people.

Above all, the values of the leader must be noble and other-directed. If not there will be an Adolf Hitler instead of an Aurelius the philosopher-emperor of Rome, or a Gandhi.

Charismatic leaders constantly refine and take their DED to higher energy levels. That energy level is superior to even charisma and more lasting too. Charismatic leaders possess a high and refined level of self-belief. They are able to relate personally to others. Personal admiration is the hallmark of loyal followers.

The force they exert on the others is thus not only electrifying but also magnetic at ever-increasing levels of cumulative perfection. Such leaders have an uncanny ability to scan and read the environment. They are extremely good at picking up the pulse of the people around them. Their words and action are thus tailored for the situation and to the individual in it. But doing so, they often change the situation itself.

What the others think of you in this process is only secondary.

When I was young, the old regarded me as an outrageous young fellow,
and now that I am old the young regard me as an outrageous old fellow.

— Galileo Galilei

BIOT-SAVART LAW

The magnetic flux density near a long, straight conductor is directly proportional to the current in the conductor, inversely proportional to the distance from the conductor.

A GOOD CONDUCTOR TRANSMITS ENERGY IN A MYRIAD OF its forms. A good leader must also be a good conductor of 'energy' in all its positive forms within an organization. You must therefore transmit your individual energies into the team and harness that of the team to achieve organizational vision and mission. You must not hinder the flow of energy across the organization but facilitate the same.

For this to happen, you must be at an optimal level of proximity with the team and the significant others in particular. You must not distance yourself from the team. Yet, you must not micro-manage either. Involvement in diurnal decisions and activities would turn out to be an avoidable interference.

The 'magnetism' or charisma that is a necessary ingredient of good leadership varies inversely with excess control and excessive involvement of the leader in the team's well-defined and routine activities. It is directly proportional to the freedom the leader gives to the team and the aloofness maintained from everyday operational decisions. Too much of familiarity and proximity dilutes the charisma.

A strand of enigma is always a part of leadership personality. Richard Branson, the flamboyant British entrepreneur displays such a passion for life and living every movement of it to its fullest. He sees life as something that includes livelihood but also extends beyond its confines.

Since 1985 Branson has been making record-breaking attempts by boat and hot air balloon. He has achieved several distance and speed records. Even a launch of a new business ventures is unique. While many in business may call it unconventional, it is just living passionately extended to business for Branson.

Exceptional leaders always have an aura of enigma around them. A certain mistique around them adds to their personal magnetism. There is always something mysterious, puzzling and unpredictable about them.

Enigmatic leaders often appear to be a jigsaw puzzle with the few pieces missing. They cannot be defined easily or categorized into a particular stereotype. This process is the common quality enigmatic leaders share when they perform diverse roles. Steve Jobs for example is known as a talented scientist, an ethical strategist and a management guru. Everybody knows everything about an enigmatic leader, and yet they know nothing about what he or she is. Their simplicity and straightforwardness at times are perplexingly disarming.

The qualities of enigma and charisma of a leader are two sides of the same coin. There is a very thin line dividing the two. More often than not, charisma and enigma overlap and are the cause and effect of each other.

The stoically ruthless 'Neutron' Jack Welch who shut unprofitable companies without battering an eyelid was also intensely emotional when it comes to skill development of GE's employees. He passionately invested millions in training and development of leaders within GE at all levels.

Soichiro Honda, the workaholic mechanic, was also an incorrigible jester. His antics included dancing on a table during an important meeting with potential investors. The shrewd taskmaster Dhirubhai Ambani, who is known to measure achievement in terms of money earned, was utterly benevolent and compassionate even at the cost of vital official work when the situation so demanded. He is once said to have put his own car at the disposal of a clerk working in his office when his wife fell ill suddenly.

Narayana Murthy's chauffeur has shares in Infosys, which are worth lakhs of rupees. And what is more, he is not disturbed by his boss on holidays. Murthy, the founder of Infosys, is known to use public transportation on Sundays since he does not know how to drive. Yet, when it comes to results, he has no favourites. An obscure young man may give an idea that would be better than that of your own top managers. The former would win, yet no one loses.

'They all shake hands and go for lunch', he once said. It may sound stoic, yet it's intensely personal too. That's the power and charm of enigma. Yet another example of an enigmatic leader is Andy Grove, the penniless Hungarian Jew who immigrated to the US and went on to become the CEO of Intel, and more importantly one of the most loved business leaders of our times. Enigmatic military leaders include the likes of Hannibal, Shaka Zulu, Josip Tito and General Patton.

KIRCHOFF'S LOOP RULE

The sum of all charges around a closed loop is equal to zero.

THERE IS THIS JOKE ABOUT A GRADUATE FROM A TOP management school being taken to a circular room and asked being to sit in a corner. It is said that he did earnestly try to do so and for quite some time until the truth dawned on him. Many leaders often think that their deputies are moving ahead with the organizational agenda fully imbibed within them. Thus they also assume that their teammates are fully in tune with the vision, values and objectives of the organization. Alas, that's not often the case. They may indeed be moving, but in circles. Energy must be channelled forward. It must surge ahead and set a trial for the others to follow in this process. Often it moves through pathless lands creating the path. Energy without constancy and consistency of purpose is a closed loop. The levels of net energy of those under its influence will therefore be zero, and so shall the results of its exertion.

In the realm of thought, the energy spent on arguments or debates without a clear picture as to their end leads to circular reasoning. It could also be that the conclusion is already decided and the debate is just a façade of organizational democracy and collective decision making. Such a situation is a closed loop—one where ideas that are exchanged neither energize nor empower.

Real leaders create open-loop conditions in their organizations where divergence of ideas are in fact encouraged. The individual energy thus becomes cumulative synergy, as will be evident in the pages that follow.

LAWS OF REFLECTION AND REFRACTION
SNELL'S LAW

It establishes the relationship between the path taken by a ray of light as it moves from one medium to another and the refractive indices of the two media.

LIGHT IS A FORM OF ENERGY THAT ILLUMINATES. IT POINTS the way. This is the illuminative role of ideas. In life you must reflect upon what comes to you as an idea. At times you must refract it too. Often ideas come to you from a wide array of sources. You will be told, you will infer, you will deduce and you will instinctively know, for thus do ideas come. Some seep in gently, some slither in unnoticed, some arrive after much deliberations, while others pop up unannounced. When ideas thus arrive in and when you communicate your ideas out, they may not be an exact replica of each other. The very same idea could be different when it comes in and goes out. This is the case when ideas are communicated between individuals. An exquisitely shaped pot comes out of raw formless clay. A raw idea can be turned within you into a fabulous paradigm of thought and action. Something similar happens when you receive ideas and thoughts of others. A tiny egg becomes a larva. The larva changes to a pupa, and the pupa to a beautiful butterfly. So is it with the metamorphosis of ideas. The source of ideas are thus broadly of two types: (i) Those involving the self within, without another individual actually communicating it to you. You must be cautious as to its source and seek to understand if it is factual or a fanciful whim. (ii) That which is communicated by others to you. You must make a little space in your mind, a little openness for being sensitive and receptive to such things.

When you communicate ideas or receive ideas from others, the path of illumination of those ideas is through a medium. The medium is the word, letter and gesture.

As light tends to refract when moving from one medium to another, so does the purport and content of an idea. Refraction may augment ideas and add to their value. Yet at times it may also result in unintended and unwanted distortion. An idea or a message has a chance of getting refracted during the process of communication leading to adverse results. A classic example is what came to be known as the charge of the Light Brigade during the Crimean War in 1854. A senior British officer misinterpreted an order and led a suicidal charge against Russian guns. This incident even became the subject of a famous poem by Alfred Tennyson titled 'The Charge of the Light Brigade'.

A good idea or concept can likewise be distorted into its undesirable form. The chemical LSD was initially intended to be a pain reliever. However, Albert Hofmann, who first synthesized it himself, contributed in turning it into a highly addictive psychotropic drug.

Let's take another example. William S. Halsted is even today considered by many to be the most innovative, influential and visionary surgeons that America has ever produced. He was a pioneer and leader in his field. One of his many creations was the chemical called ether that is used as a general anaesthetic. Halsted himself almost became addicted while experimenting for a method to perform painless surgeries. $E = MC^2$ is a great formula if rightfully used for ending the global energy crisis. A lump of plutonium can light up a city for months. If it is misused as a neutron bomb, it could blow up the very city in a matter of seconds.

Pay heed therefore to the source of ideas. Seek their natural direction and then reflect or refract them as necessity demands. This is one of the qualities that adds to leadership magnetism. This idea is dealth with elaborately in the following chapter.

FAMOUS WORDS OF CLAUSIUS

Energy cannot itself pass from a colder to a hotter object.

YOUR VISION, MISSION AND IDEALS BY THEMSELVES cannot pass on to the others as if by magic. Even charisma must be carefully cultivated and communicated at times. Charisma in a closet would not befit a leader nor benefit a follower. You must make the right effort to transfer your energy to your team.

The level of energy and types of energy is often relative. The difference between the hot and the cold is one of degree. There are no opposites in life but only difference in degree. Even the relatively 'colder' or less enthused person has something to offer to the more enthused one. The former can also be a sterling counter-example or an anti-role model to the latter. You must juxtapose the two in a manner that those of the former type are inspired and those who belong to the latter category become more aware and confident of their latent positive attributes.

There is a stanza in the Rig Veda that reads as follows:

Samani va akutih Samana
Hrdayani vah Samanamastu vo
Mano yatha vah sahahesati.

It means: 'Common be your intentions, common be your hearts, common be your thoughts, so that there may be thorough unity among you.'

A leader must put into action what was envisaged in the Rig Veda and bring about synergy of energy, so to say.

PLANCK THEORY

Radiant energy can be emitted or absorbed only in discrete amounts called quanta and not in a continuous stream.

YOU MAY BE FULL OF ENERGY BUT ITS RADIATION OUTWARD is not always continuous and constant. Therefore, the success or otherwise of leadership depends a great deal on 'followership' also. If not, the energy radiating out of a leader would then be like the rays of the sun blocked by dark clouds. The inspiration that the leader ought to or attempts to provide would be insipid and distorted.

The leader is what he or she is because others are not so. You must therefore at best instinctively or in the least intellectually know that the actual impact your energy will have on your team is in discreet quanta. It will be in distinct interactions and instances, albeit interwoven. The effect it would have on your teammates will not be the same for all individuals constituting the team. This is because all your teammates are not of the same personality type. Expecting everyone to have the same ideas and believe in them with similar intensity and passion is unscientific and not founded in reality.

The energy in the form of inspiration that you ooze out will not at once and as such enter into the minds and hearts of your teammates. Depending on their personality type and state of mind, it will be absorbed, understood and imbibed in discreet amounts and that too intermittently by each individual.

A leader must feel the pulse of his people and access their ideas, emotions and motivation levels correctly. When a leader assumes too much about his people and begins to think that his ideas and emotions will be exactly the same as that of the others, he tends to get increasingly delinked from his people. When this happens, the most brilliant and successful leaders fail miserably. Alexander led his soldiers through a blaze of battles and victories across continents. Yet, he appointed Harpalos, a coward and an unscrupulous character, as his finance controller, much against the advice of his friends and generals. Later, Harpalos not only swindled huge amounts of money from the army's war treasure but also instigated a rebellion against Alexander, his very benefactor. After conquering Persepolis, Alexander's soldiers across the rank and file wanted to go back home to Macedon. They were physically exhausted after a long expedition of over a decade. They simply wanted to go home to their families. Alexander addressed his troops and gave inspiring speeches to goad them to go on.

After the fierce battles of Sogdiana and Bactriana, the gap between Alexander and his soldiers widened. This reached a point of near mutiny when Alexander reached India in 326 BC. This time Alexander's eloquent and inspiring speeches fell flat. His men no longer shared his vision or had the same levels of motivation to continue conquering continents endlessly. Alexander, the great warrior and leader, was as demanding on himself as he was with his men. He shared their hardships of long campaigns and also the glory and gold of the conquests. He did lead by example. Yet, he did not realize that the virtue of leading by example has its inherent limitations when too much is assumed by the leader on behalf of his followers.

Business leaders of legendary proportions too met the same fate. Henry Ford was as noble and kind man as he was shrewd in business decisions. His company Ford Motor Co.

was doing phenomenally well. He achieved his vision of making the automobile affordable to the very workers who make it. He often called his employees members of his extended family. All was well till he turned too paternalistic and began determining what the workers at the company needed or did not need. All thought and emotive processes turned to flow one way – from Henry Ford to the others.

Henry Ford was an icon to many working-class people. He offered higher wages than others in the same sector and encouraged African Americans and people with disabilities to join his company. However, during the Great Depression of 1930s retrenchment was rampant. Workers everywhere in the US organized themselves into unions to protect their rights. Ford Motor Co. had a union too, yet Henry Ford believed that he knew what was best for the workers than the workers themselves. He refused to recognize the union. This led to the historic and infamous clash between the security personnel and the protesting workers. Dozens of workers were beaten up ruthlessly in the presence of national media. Henry Ford's credibility among his employees and perhaps his confidence level as their benevolent leader received a severe setback.

Walt Disney, another business legend, fell prey to a similar situation. Walt Disney too was a benevolent leader. Yet, he too began to take his employees for granted. The 'they all think and feel as I do' syndrome led to a workers' strike. Walt Disney was forced to leave the country on a 'goodwill tour' abroad while his younger brother handled the situation.

RAMAN EFFECT

When light of a single wavelength passes through a transparent medium some of the light is scattered.

THE ILLUMINATING ENERGY OF THE LEADER BECOMES the *power* to inspire desired and intended ideas in the others and the *force* that would generate action in a desired direction at a predetermined rate. Thus, your energy can be, and at times *must* be of different wavelengths.

This is because the people you lead are a mixture of three broad categories of mind-being states – the Vata, the Pitta, and the Kapha, as discussed earlier. The same wavelength of illuminative or invigorative energy will not have the same, and even less a similar, intensity of impact on all of them. Thus, when addressing a team , energy must be broken down to different wavelengths to reach recipients who will be of different emotional and intellectual types. The nature of the medium used to reach out to the others is also vital, although the latter has more to do with the time factor than the qualitative import of the message itself. Remember, the message itself has the energy of the leader inherent in it. The message is the primordial energy in its overt expression.

A much too rigid medium, the bureaucratic type, will diminish the energy and thus its potential force. A much too transparent medium on the other hand will only end in diluting and scattering it.

TYNDALL EFFECT

If a strong beam of light energy passes through a colloidal solution placed in dark, the path of the beam is illuminated by a bluish visible light.

AT TIMES, A LEADER FACES A MIXTURE OF MINDS IN A colloidal and fluid state. Similar mind-states in a group and that too at the lower rungs of knowledge and commitment are a daunting task for a leader to enlighten. Such a group mind is in a state of dark ignorance, opaque to reality and truth. This state is symptomatic of the *tamo-guna* (as has been defined in earlier pages). You can still reach such minds and teach them. The illuminating energy of the leader as a blue streak can penetrate areas of ignorance and leave a trail. This is not just a symbolic figure of speech.

As it was explained and established in the prologue to this book, the human body emits energy in the form of fields called auras. They are known by different names in the medical systems of Asia. Modern science has found evidence of its existence. All human auras are interconnected and are interdependent. A Kirlian photograph is a photograph made by high voltage electricity. It is named after Semyon Kirlian, a scientist who discovered accidentally that when an object on a photographic plane is subjected to higher voltage electricity, electric fields are created which in turn create an image on the photographic plane. Kirlian photography forms an interesting part of parapsychology where 'auras' generated by human body are photographed. When made visual with techniques such as Kirlian photography, the auras are found to be of many colours, just as the ancients have said. The royal blue aura is found prominently in people who have found their chosen path in life and have the ability to lead people on that path. They have the 'blue streak' as they lead.

FERMAT'S PRINCIPLE

When light energy travels from
point A to point B,
it follows a path which takes the least time.

ENERGY IN A LEADER IS OF MANY FORMS. AS HEAT, IT ignites and spurs action. As light, it illuminates minds and guides them. As sound it communicates and instructs, as electric current it charges up the minds and hearts. As magnetism it attracts and bonds.

The energy of a leader is thus path-breaking and path-finding. Path-breaking leadership involves originality and innovation. The path-finding aspect of leadership is characterized by discovering a path that exists but was hitherto unknown. The leader treads on uncharted territory and leaves a trail for others to follow. When the energy of a leader is of the nature of light or in its illuminating mode, it naturally takes the minimal amount of time to reach its intended recipient(s) or destination. The revelation born out of the leader is instantaneous. Its effect appears to be spontaneous. Andy Grove, the CEO of Intel, coined the word 'Strategic Inflection Points'. In his book *Only the Paranoid Survive* he describes the periods of sudden and massive upheaval that affects the organization's competitive position and ushers in a thorough introspection of its strategies and internal processes. A strategic inflection point creates a massive shift in the way business is conducted.

Let's take the captivating story of Sunil Mittal, Chairman and CEO Bharati Enterprises. The first strategic inflection point that he encountered was his failed attempt in getting a Maruti Suzuki agency in Ludhiana. It made him look for other business opportunities. Sunil Mittal saw the massive power shortages Ludhiana was reeling under and began importing portable generators. He made huge profits. Then came the second strategic inflection point in the form of government notification banning import of power generators. Overnight Sunil Mittal's livelihood came to an abrupt end. He began travelling. At one electronic fair at Taipei his hawk eye landed on the push button telephone and he began importing push button telephones to India.

In 1992 mobile telephony was thrown open to the private sector. Mittal plunged into forming a consortium and Bharti Telecom was born. Then came another strategic inflection point in the form of a failure. Bharti had applied for four circles but then a decision was taken by the government to allot one license only to each competing company. Sunil Mittal turned this to his advantage and focused on only one circle with all the resources he could muster instead of diluting them by investing in many circles. 'We lost but to win,' he says today.

The going was great and customers were growing. Ironically, this success resulted in another strategic inflection point. There was a need for huge manpower to keep up with the scale of operations. This was when Sunil Mittal made a 'leap into faith' by adopting outsourcing as a business model much to the bewilderment of industry experts and fellow businessmen. This model was a stupendous success. Mittal is an example of turning strategic inflection points to breakthrough opportunities by a highly optimal energy flow.

However, there may be intervening factors that affect the rate of movement along a path depending on the medium through which the illuminative and guiding energy of the leader travels. This is where Huygens' Wave Theory comes in.

4

Personal Magnetism

The Power of Attraction, Appeal and Charisma

LAW OF MAGNETISM

Magnetism is the property or quality of an object or an entity revealed as the power to attract. It is the manifestation of the force in nature which is seen in a magnet.
When objects made up of metals such as iron are in constant proximity with a magnet, the power of magnetism is built up within them.

MAGNETISM IS ALSO A FORM OF ENERGY. IT IS THE POSITIVE energy exuded by visionary leaders, seers, and people of virtue. It has a natural propensity to attract those who aspire to be successful, good and noble human beings. Being materially successful on the one hand and being good and noble at the same time is not a contradiction in terms even in this era of Kali (Kaliyuga) where ruthless games of deception and deceit reign supreme. When means are disregarded, the ends at best bring fleeting gains and pleasures. With goodness and nobility comes lasting success and happiness.

Personal magnetism is never conferred. It is either achieved or acquired, often painstakingly. It is achieved by skilful and diligent nurturing of personal traits that foster the power of magnetism. It is acquired by being in the company of the good and the noble among people whatever be their station or calling in life. Iron, when in constant contact with a magnet, itself turns into one.

A sterling example for the above can be found in the persona of Dr Govindappa Venkataswamy, the founder of Aravind Eye Hospitals. The organization has till date given sight to over 13 million people. It has set global records in the number of cataract surgeries performed per day. What started off as a small 12-bed facility is today a group of ultra-modern hospitals.

Aravind has set global benchmarks in cost leadership in the eye care industry. On an average a cataract surgery costs $1,650 in the US, whereas at Aravind it works out to $10 only. Intra-ocular lenses cost around $100–150 in the US, whereas Aravind is able to manufacture and sell them at merely $4–6 per piece. Aravind is also a pioneer in a system where the 'haves' subsidize 'have-nots'. The charges collected from the rich go a long way into subsidizing the treatment of the poor.

G. Venkataswamy was born in a small village near Madurai in Tamil Nadu. His village was remote and underdeveloped, and there were no schools in it. As a little boy, Venkataswamy had to walk over three miles to the neighbouring village to attend school. The school did not even have a blackboard. Students used to collect sand from a nearby riverbed, spread it on the mud floor and use it as a slate. He also had to help his father with his farm work and his mother with the household chores.

Despite all difficulties, he proved to be a brilliant student in school and college. He completed his Obstetrics in 1944 and served as a doctor in the Army Corps during the World War II. After the war, he was affected by rheumatoid arthritis, which permanently disfigured his fingers. He underwent great physical and emotional pain and suffering. He could not practise his medical profession because of his handicap.

Then in 1950 he met Shri Aurobindo and was immensely impressed by him. The spiritual saint had a magnetic influence on the young doctor, who realized that life is a journey of the embodied spirit towards Godhead. A statement by Shri Aurobindo is the first thing you read when you click the 'About Us' icon in Aravind's homepage. It reads: 'Spirituality allows the divine force to work through each of us for a greater good.'

With new hope and determination Dr Venkataswamy joined the medical school again in 1955 and specialized in Ophthalmology (a branch of medicine dealing with the eye). He even designed special instruments to fit his disfigured fingers. In 1956 he became Head of the Department, Madurai Medical College, and shot to fame by performing 100 cataracts in one day.

Most visionary stories of success end with retirement. With Dr Venkataswamy it was another beginning that made him a legend. In 1978 he mortgaged his only house and started a small eye clinic with 12 beds. Today the Aravind Eye Care System has become a case study in both philanthropy and entrepreneurship.

C.K. Prahalad, a leading management 'guru', states that Aravind earns over 200 per cent returns on capital employed. According to him, it is one of the best market-driven companies on earth. It is serving the most ignored segment of the market – the poor. Other studies have shown that 70 per cent of surgeries at Aravind are free. And yet Aravind maintains a 40 per cent profit margin.

The 'persona' of Dr Venkataswamy made a decisive difference in Aravind's spectacular success. He took personal responsibility in realizing a vision. He organized eye camps and awareness programmes in rural areas. Brilliant doctors volunteer to work at Aravind for low salaries or for no salary at all in some cases.

The management guru Jim Collins calls him a level-5 leader in an article published in the *Harvard Business Review*. The first four levels have to do with reaching targets, getting things done, setting the agenda, motivating people, etc. A level-5 leader is the one who goes through and also rises even above these levels. Such a leader ascribes his own success to others and not to himself. If that is not possible, then to a higher consciousness. All his actions are in alignment with this state of being.

Dr Venkataswamy's persona as a visionary, a spectacular achiever, a social worker, an ascetic of sorts is perhaps best reflected in a verse in the Gita:

Yatra yogishvara Krishno, yatra Partho dhanur–dharah
Tatra srir vijayo bhutir, dhruva nitir matir mama

'Wherever there is the "yogi" Krishna (symbolizing the state of mind aligned with a higher consciousness or purpose), with Arjuna with his 'bow and arrows' (symbolizing correct action), there you shall find firmly established fortune, victory, power and virtue.' The very words of DrVenkataswamy sums it all up. When asked about his social commitment and service to humanity, he smiled and said, 'It is ourselves we are helping. It is ourselves we are healing.' That's personal magnetism at its best. Dr Venkataswamy passed away recently, but his team of doctors, paramedics, administrative staff and supportive staff continue to be swayed by his magnetism.

Magnetism and charisma are closely related to one another. Magnetism of an individual is not only the power of attraction but also the power of transformation. Individuals with magnetic personality change attitudes, thoughts and behaviour of others. Gautama, the Buddha, had such power which could transform even the worst of criminals. The parable of Angulimala from the Theravada tradition is an interesting example.

There was once a thief who was popularly known as Angulimala because he killed his victims and made a garland of their thumbs. The king of the land was very concerned and began to organize his entire army to kill Angulimala. Meanwhile, the Buddha was walking through the very jungle where Angulimala reigned. When Angulimala saw the Buddha he ordered him to stop, but the Buddha kept walking.

So Angulimala ran and ran towards the Buddha, but he could not catch up with him. He became so weak that he could not run any further. Then he shouted at the Buddha 'Stop! Stand still.'

'I stand still Angulimala evermore, for I am merciful to all living beings, but you are merciless to living beings. Therefore, I stand still and you stand not still,' the Buddha said with a meaningful smile.

These words and the look at the Buddha's face was enough to overpower the negative *karma* of Angulimala. He fell at the feet of the Buddha and became his disciple.

The king who went to the monastery to pay homage to the Buddha was amazed at the transformation that had taken place in a man like Angulimala by the sheer magnetism and positive *karma* of the Buddha.

COMPTON EFFECT

Wavelength of electromagnetic radiation increases on being scattered by electrons. Wavelength is the distance between two points (Peak or crest) of a wave of energy to the next corresponding one. Energy is thus radiated outward.

RADIATION IS THE DISSEMINATION, OR SPREADING out of energy through space. The energy within a leader must likewise spread out to his team, even though they may be geographically or spatially separated. The reach of the leader transcends boundaries – physical, cultural and psychological. At times, the 'reach' surpasses the acknowledged grasp. Physical proximity is not a rigid precondition to the energy transference process from a leader to his or her team. Not everyone among the millions of freedom fighters had actually seen Mahatma Gandhi in person. Yet, his magnetism inspired them on the path of *satyagraha*. The same was the passion inspired by other leaders of legendary proportions such as Abraham Lincoln, Mother Teresa, Martin Luther King and Rosa Parks. In the world of science, there was Albert Einstein, Newton and Oppenheimer. In business there are many, some of whom find mention in this book in different contexts.

Today, the transference of magnetism through long distance is made easier by advances in communication technology. We are familiar with the TV series *Charlie's Angels* of the 1970s. Charlie is the off-site leader who delegates, directs and motivates his team through a speakerphone. Today this has moved from the world of fiction to that of fact. In a millennium replete with complexity at all levels of human interaction and convergence of technologies, you have a unique opportunity to usher in a convergence of vision, values and goals of the organization.

That's when the team gets into sync with your 'wavelength'. Your image and persona without dilution and distortion. When that happens, you are at the threshold of becoming a legend.

5

Stress and Conflict Management

Beating Stress and Benefiting from Polarity

THE LAWS OF THERMODYNAMICS

(Zeroth Law of Thermodynamics)

If two thermodynamic systems are in thermal equilibrium with a third, they are also in thermal equilibrium with each other.

PRINCIPLES OF THERMODYNAMIC SYSTEMS

Open Systems

Such systems have permeable boundaries. They display adaptability. They sustain growth and serve their parent environment.
Energy is drawn from space continually.

Closed Systems

These are characterized by restricted laws.
Energy is expended continuously.

YOU ARE A BUNDLE OF IDEAS, IDEALS, PASSIONS, EMOTIONS all of which are expressions of energy in different forms. Combinations of these make you temperamentally what you are. By anger, the cosmic energy with which you are naturally in harmony is disturbed.

Diametrically opposite emotions such as hate–love, vanity–humility, wrath–compassion, sadness–joy, etc. are all in a dynamic combination with one emotion reigning over the other. This produces dynamic instability. This 'soup' of emotions boils in the cauldron of your being. When negative emotions reign supreme and there is mutual animosity between two individuals, try to find a third person with whom the opposite of your emotion is prominent. By thus doing so, the two perceived rivals will also reach a state of equilibrium. In short, the third person will act as a mediating force. He or she will enable the two individuals at odds with each other in realigning their energies.

During the massive strike in 1974 at Disney Studios neither the union leaders nor Walt Disney relented. Walt Disney held on to his views adamantly. The matter had turned into a huge ego problem for him and the union. His younger brother stepped in as a mediator even as the strike cascaded up. Walt Disney was eased off from the country on a 'goodwill' world tour while his brother sorted out the matter. The egos of both sides were not hurt and the issue was settled amicably.

A similar mediator rescue was enacted during the historic workers' agitation against Rockefeller. His son

Rockefeller Jr stepped in and sorted out the issue. More recently, we have seen industry bigwigs serve as third-party mediators to make the split between the Ambanis as peaceful as possible.

More recently, a judge in the Supreme Court of India asked the disputing Ambani Brothers to approach their mother to sort out their differences. By being in equilibrium with the third party, two individuals automatically achieve equilibrium with each other.

The mediator can not only serve as a buffer between two or more personalities at loggerheads but can also play a creative role in proactively resolving a conflict.

If you are agitated or in disharmony with someone, find a third person with whom both of you are in harmony and at peace with. Thus shall harmony set itself between the two of you. Be yourself the third person to set harmony between the other two if so required.

Your own internal energy increases if you absorb it from different sources while not expending it without a purpose on people and tasks. Prioritize its usage. Invest it for the right purpose and for the right reasons. If not, the transformation that your energy undergoes or intends to inspire in others will be ineffective and for no tangible benefit. You thus fritter it and squander it away.

Even top-notch leaders end up doing so. Alfred Solan is arguably one of the top business leaders of this century. He became the Chairman of General Motors Corporation in 1957. He showed his skill and dexterity in managing diverse operations at General Motors. Solan was also the founding father of concepts such as 'planned obsolescence', 'statistical financial analysis' in day-to-day operations. He established a pricing structure of different automobile brands of General Motors such as Chevrolet, Pontiac, Cadillac, Buick and Oldsmobile in such a manner that they did not complete (compete) or cannibalize each other. The customers could scale up the models as their purchasing power increased. As the long-term President and Chairman of General Motors (GM) he built the company and his own reputation to legendary proportions.

When there was clash of ideas between a young engineer named Charles Kettering and the heads of other departments over a new model of an engine, Solan tried to 'manage' the immediate conflict instead of 'leading' the team forward together. Instead of encouraging an interactive debate on the issue, he created a separate department to independently develop the engine under Kettering.

The crisis was over and everyone happily went back to their respective work. Years later, in his autobiography titled *My Years with GM* Solan confesses that he made a big mistake. So much energy was expended and yet it was all for nothing.

KIRCHOFF'S LAW

At any given instant, the sum of the values of all the energy flowing towards a point is equal to the sum of the valve of all energies flowing away from the point.

ENTROPY

Energy spontaneously tends to, if so allowed, flow from being concentrated in one place to becoming diffused.
If intervening obstacles are removed, energy spreads outwards.

AS WITH MANY OTHER LAWS AND POSTULATES OF science, this law too is in the borderline area of science and spirituality. The ancient Chinese philosophers believed that the whole universe is made up of two opposing yet dynamically interacting principles – the *yin* and the *yang*. The *yins* and *yangs* operate in the universe with ruthless precision. Even as you are achieving, there is a potential and notional loss, and vice-versa. A thing that is desirable has in itself dormant aspects that are undesirable, and the converse is likewise true. A person or an object has value, a part of which is posited from outside and a part emanates from the nature of one's own being. Since values that are ascribed differ in degree, differences of opinion must be respected. Gain or loss, winning or losing must also be viewed as *yins* and *yangs* each containing the other within.

Excellence in life is thus a journey, with lifetime purpose being the destination and success or failure being mere signposts along the way. The art and science of skilful leadership consists in acknowledging the constant dialectic of the opposites and taking a detached view of both. With such detachment comes the ability to enhance the good and endure the bad. As a swan that sucks up pure water from a muddy pond, you will get the best out of a hopelessly murky situation.

As Marcus Aurelius, the philosopher king of ancient Rome, writes in conclusion of his book *Meditations* 'pass on then with a smiling face under the watchful smile of Him who bides you go'.

In an overt conflict situation open collusion of attitudes, ideas and thoughts is a distinct possibility. When two individuals are involved in such a situation it often degenerates into a clash of inflated egos. That is indeed negative to those involved in the collusion and for the significant others be it at workplace or at home. The two 'bodies' or individuals who clash need not be at similar levels of power, authority or responsibility. This difference of being 'bigger' or 'smaller' does not matter insofar as the effect of the clash is concerned. One or the other may turn out to be a winner in such a collusion, but that is not enduring victory. It is at best a momentary thing.

The *momentum* of those involved in the collusion will nevertheless remain the same. They will continue to nurse a grudge, wrath and anger against one another. Their attitudes will remain as they were before the collusion, if not grow more virulent. The unnoticed first casuality of such a collusion between two individuals is peace and harmony at the workplace or at home as the case may be. A collusion rooted in ego is bound to be destructive and self-destructive too. Like the aftermath of a nuclear war, there will ultimately be no winners.

Our psychological sense of time is based on this law. It is the crux of our past observations, experiences and our expectations of the future based on them. Air does not rush into a tyre. Toothpaste does not flow back into the tube. For this to happen energy would have to be increasingly concentrated instead of spreading out.

Things don't have any tendency in themselves towards macro disorder. When energy flow spreads out, the entropy at the micro-level decreases.

You must not only let his energy spread out naturally but also unlock the pent-up positive energies of his teammates. You must facilitate the team to move ahead freely. This is much like a parent who, while watching a toddler learn to walk, removes objects over which the child could tumble upon.

For this to happen, the ego expressed in the word 'I' must be set aside. You will thus kindle potential energy that results in a surge of the kinetic energy. Your magnetism will further be enhanced. As positive energy is given out, personal magnetism increases.

OHMIC LOSS OR JOULE HEATING

Ohmic loss is the loss of energy when current flows through a resistance due to conversion into heat.
At an atomic level, it becomes Joule heating.
Electrons colliding within an atom in a conductor transfer their momentum,
thereby increasing the kinetic energy in the system.

THERE WILL BE RESISTANCE TO THE FLOW OF YOUR IDEAS. There will be opposition when you try to translate your ideas into action. There will also be impediments when you begin to act or cause action. This tends to deplete energy. Do not let this resistance turn to confrontation or a clash at a personal level. When Jeff Bezos founded Amazon.com in 1994, he was criticized and ridiculed by many in the industry. Business pundits predicted that the fledgling venture would fail instantly. Amazon's original goal was to sell anything, starting with books.

Many believed that the rival website launched by the established publisher Barnes and Noble in 1997 would deliver the death-blow to Amazon.com. Bezos was unfazed and as optimistic as ever. He held on to his ground even when Amazon shares dropped from $100 to $6 as a result of these criticisms. Bezos had an uncanny ability to quantify data and statistics into his marketing and business goals. Under his stewardship, Amazon.com flourished and quickly became a market leader in the online retail segment. Bezos made it into the Forbes list of the world's wealthiest people and he is worth as estimated $5.7 billion today.

Be level-headed. With you being thus, your detractors and rivals will only burn up their energy in vain. When theirs is depleted, yours will paradoxically become more potent by absorbing into itself effects of the energy the rivals have expended. At another level a reasonable degree of moderated fiction between ideas is healthy for interpersonal relationships and also organizational growth. Controlled and channelized conflict has its positive benefits in personal and professional life.

ARCHIMEDES' PRINCIPLE OF FLOTATION

The apparent loss in weight of a body immersed in a fluid is equal to the weight of the displaced fluid.
The upward force that enables the object to float is called buoyancy.

PRINCIPLES OF STRESS AND STRAIN

Stress is defined as force per unit area.
It has the same units as pressure, since pressure is one special variety of stress.
However, stress is a much more complex entity than pressure because it varies both with direction and with the surface it acts on.
Strain is defined as the amount of deformation an object experiences compared to its original size and shape.

IF YOU CANNOT LEAD YOURSELF, HOW CAN YOU PRESUME that you can possibly lead others? If you yourself sink, how can you expect to hold the others and keep them afloat?

Buoyancy or the force which keeps a body afloat is equal to the weight of fluid it displaces, so simple yet so profound. In life, as in science, the greatest of truths are often the simplest. An iron nail sinks in water but a gigantic ship made of iron stays afloat. This is because the ship displaces more water than its own weight by being so shaped.

It takes authenticity and a passion for truth to distinguish what is essential and what is non-essential in life. It takes common sense to eliminate the non-essentials. Much of the sublime wisdom garnered by mankind is just common sense at its core. Yet we assume our views and attitudes must be as perceivably complex as the world we live in. Simplicity makes one insecure, for, it makes one confront the truth and the laws of your own being. You are unmasked! You therefore attempt to create complexity and concoct the powerlessness of your own freewill. That is the wall behind which you hide.

The more irrelevant and non-essential things and thoughts you eliminate from your life the more will there be relevant and worthy ones left. The more the buoyancy, the more easily and effortlessly can you stay afloat in the tumultuous waters of daily life and sail along the worldly sea. Thus you shall soon reach calm waters. Thus you shall sail placidly even as winds and waves lash out again.

It is often the trivialities and ultimately inconsequential things that are in the saddle and ride mankind. Many studies by leading research institutions have revealed that between 80 to 90 per cent of all personal and interpersonal problems are attitudinal in nature. A change in attitude will give scope to viewing situations as they are. The preferable will thus win over the fleeting pleasurable. Thus you voyage along to your destination in life controlling the sails if not the direction of the wind.

There are different types of stress. Eustress is positive stress. It inspires creativity and motivates an individual to complete the task in hand to its perfection. The next type of stress is distress, which is a negative form of stress. It results in fear, anger, frustration and remorse. Stress in excess results in anxiety and mental agony. Understress is another type of condition when an individual is not challenged enough. The individual feels his capabilities and ideas are not utilized to the fullest. Lack of positive stress is also a characteristic of understress. What results are waywardness, dullness and boredom. The next type of stress is overstress. This occurs when the individual feels the demands being made on him and those that he is making upon himself are too much to bear. Too much of workload, too many deadlines and too little time for personal growth and the family result in overstress.

The leader has the ability to convert three kinds of negative stress into positive stress. Nelson Mandela was imprisoned on Robin Island for 18 long years. On Robin Island he was forced to perform hard labour in a lime quarry. Conditions in the prison were inhuman. Mandela was a D-group prisoner, which was the lowest ranking among prisoners. He was allowed only one visitor and one letter every six months. Anybody else would have cracked at such a situation given the psychological torture by prison authorities specially meted out to Mandela. Yet, Mandela enrolled with the University of London and received the Degree of Bachelor of Laws while in prison. Robin Island, which was intended to stress him out and break him in fact strengthened his determination and will. Robin Island became the crucible which transformed him. His charisma and magnetism increased day by day in prison with his dignified poise and determined non-violent defiance. Mandela was able to transform even the ruthless jail authorities and became the unquestioned leader of other inmates.

A similar situation transformed Shri Aurobindo. He was kept in a small cell at the Alipore Jail in a solitary confinement for an entire year after which he was found not guilty and acquitted. This one-year meant to break him brought about a miraculous transformation. Sri Aurobindo redirected his mind and will on the divine conscience. It was a period of intense *sadhana*. It was here that he had the experience of Supra-self and the oneness of all beings. He went into jail as a man and came out as an enlightened saint.

Yet stress and strain in life are facts that must be audaciously and assiduously confronted. The simple law of Hooke that follows tells us how to do this.

HOOKE'S LAW

Stress within a body is directly proportional to the strain that the object exhibits.

$$\frac{stress}{strain} = constant$$

Depending on their response to stress, objects can be classified as elastic, brittle, ductile or viscous.

STRESS AND STRAIN ARE REFLECTIVE OF AND DEPENDENT on the mental state you are in. Your attitude and mindset can firstly disallow or filter outside influences that build stress within you. Secondly, even if stress is unavoidable, it need not result in strain that is the debilitating effect of stress. Strain is the symptom whose immediately precedent cause is stress. The root cause of stress is your mindset itself.

A solid-state mindset (as described in an earlier chapter) is brittle and breaks into smithereens under stress. It is characterized by rigidity and compactness. Such a state is impervious to new ideas and knowledge. When met with resistance, what results is 'all or none' situation. At the other avoidable extreme is the gaseous state in mindset. The fluid-state mindset is less rigid. It is ductile and more amenable to adaptation. It is able to cope with stress and strain more efficiently. It is able to endure stress longer and thus deal with it better.

The fluid state is able to overcome stress by also simple 'flowing past' difficult people and situations, much like a rivulet that does not try to bore through a boulder in its path but simply circumvents it. The boulder is bypassed, it is just ignored. The boulder, which is a 'solid' is indeed strong, yet it is not as superior in adaptability and movement as is a rivulet, a fluid.

As it is with rocks and rivers, so is it with the inherent nature of man. The river flows placidly in spite of things and circumstances out there. It is at ease with itself. It deflects itself around obstacles turns them into islands. Then it becomes its own undivided self again. In situations of absolute certainty and control, the solid state mindset may prevail. Alas, uncertainty is a fact of life. It paradoxically gives new meaning to life by making way for the role of your free will. The liquid state mindset will however enable you to stay on course in life just a river meanders through hills and gorges as it flows on serenely to its destination.

Success flows with the flow of the liquid-state mindset. The history of mankind is replete with such stories. Let me site just two of them from home ground.

Lakshmi Das Mittal was a farmer and witnessed the family suffer due to vagaries of weather. After harvesting, threshing takes a lot of time during which the grains would be in the open and rains would often destroy the crop. Lakshmi Das Mittal knew that the only way to solve this problem was by quicker threshing by machines. He and a friend of his designed and came up with a thresher and borrowed money from friends and relatives to make a few of them. However, the farmers who used them returned them saying that they were useless. Lakshmi Das Mittal and his friend found that curved cutters instead of straight ones were more effective.

Lakshmi Das Mittal once again borrowed money and began making 'threshers.' Slowly he diversified into making other farm instruments. The journey was far from smooth or miraculous. Then came the forays into making tractors. Today multi-utility passenger carriers are being churned out in collaboration with MG Rover (UK) by the ₹3,000 crore Sonalika Group which he is the Chairman.

That someone who could not afford a pair of spectacles, his vision and endurance became his strength. There is no laid-back attitude for people in the liquid-state mindset. There is always the flow.

It had long since come to my attention
that people of accomplishment rarely sat back and
let things happen to them.
They went out and happened to things.

— Leonardo da Vinci

DOPPLER EFFECT

A change in the observed frequency of a wave (of sound or light) occurring when the source and observer are in motion relative to each other, with the frequency increasing when the source and the observer approach each other and decreasing when they move apart.
The sound of an approaching ambulance with its siren blaring increases as it approaches the observer and fades away as it passes by.

WE EXPERIENCE THE DOPPLER EFFECT EVERY DAY. Encountering events and situations that are unpleasant is inevitable in life. Yet, many need not be endured longer than they ought to. The extraction of a tooth may be inevitable, yet the act itself lasts less than a minute. Thinking about the impending visit to the dentist a week ahead will make you live the pain over and over again. While the actual extraction may in fact be that of one molar, you would have mentally lived the agony and anxiety of a hundred being removed. Like the blaring sound of a siren approaching, many unpleasant events in life have an increasing impact on your mind as they approach you. They will all invariably pass on and even their effect will dwindle away with time. Procrastinating on the facing of the consequences of inevitable events will only make them more disturbing than they often really are. If an unpleasant event does occur, do not carry it in your mind longer than you have to. Let it pass. Don't dwell on it. Don't re-live the pain of the molar extracted once you leave the doctor's clinic.

The blaring sound of the approaching vehicle will invariably pass by. Is it not foolish to sit in the vehicle itself and lament that the distressing sound is always following you? At an even more sublime level, you may want to consider even the pleasant and pleasurable events in life as things that approach you and move away. Relish them but do not revel in them in excess. Take the best of the past and hope for the best for the future. But take each task, each situation, and each day for what it is 'here-and-now'. For, all things that approach you shall pass away leaving impressions that are for your free will to deal with.

PRINCIPLES OF EQUILIBRIUM AND ITS TYPES

Equilibrium is a state where opposing forces or tendencies neutralize each other and a state of even balance is displayed by the system/object.

UNSTABLE OR RESTLESS EQUILIBRIUM

It is the state of the system that may not be restored after the introduction of a disturbance or perturbation.

STABLE YET IMPERFECT EQUILIBRIUM

It is a condition when a slight displacement of a system is followed by its return to the original position.

ABSOLUTELY STABLE EQUILIBRIUM

It is a condition where outside disturbance or perturbation has no impact on the original condition of the system or object.

DYNAMIC EQUILIBRIUM

It is a condition when parts or aspects of the system fluctuate and change according to the external disturbance or perturbation, yet, it is in overall balance. The system or object is in relative motion yet unchanged within itself.

DAY-TO-DAY LIFE IS INDEED NOT ALWAYS A SMOOTH and unhindered journey. There will be impediments, roadblocks and potholes in your way even as you stroll or jog or more often sprint through it. Life is both a rally and a race. You need to move fast as in a race yet not so fast as to prematurely exhaust yourself. For, life is a long rally too which needs endurance.

One of the essentials of winning in this race-cum-rally is equilibrium. At the individual level it is the psycho-somatic equilibrium of the mind, emotions and body. At the professional level, it is the equilibrium of the organic entity called the team at one end and the entire organization at another.

As a corollary, a leader who is in a state of mind-emotion equilibrium is the one who can infuse the same among his teammates and get the organization into such a state as well.

Equilibrium can be of different types. It can be unstable, stable yet imperfect, stable and dynamic. As it is with science, so is it with life. And therefore, to all of you who think stable equilibrium is the best of all types, think again. Science is of facts, and so is authentic life.

An example of unstable or restless equilibrium is that of a pencil that is placed vertically on one's palm. When the support is removed, it will fall instantly. A pendulum is still and stable. But with a little tap, it starts oscillating for long, returning to its original position again. This is stable yet imperfect equilibrium. A rock by seashore that remains unmoved and unaffected by the waves and winds that lash out against it is in a state of absolutely stable equilibrium. An eagle with outstretched wings gliding in the skies far above with its sights on the earth is in a state of dynamic equilibrium.

There can be no one 'magic-bullet' method of leading people. Leadership is essentially an adaptive process. It adapts the self and enables others to adapt too. You must be aware of the differences between various types of people and situations. You must also understand how the same types of people act in different situations. This will enhance your effectiveness in interpersonal interaction and foster high levels of intellectual emotional engagement. You can thus tailor your own approach and that of the others to different situations for getting the best results.

Dhirubhai Ambani's leadership style cannot be put into a particular pigeonhole of management theory. He evolved a unique style that combined the aggressive American type entrepreneurship, the Japanese focus on technology and the shrewdness of a Gujarati businessman. He was the ideal manager of time, money and men even in non-ideal and imperfect situations.

Type of Equilibrium	*Individual Characteristics*
Unstable or Restless	Psycho-Somatic imbalance. Unsteady mind and tumultuous emotions. No conviction in beliefs and values. Easily perturbed by external influences.
Stable yet Imperfect	Psycho-Somatic balance in general. Mind and emotions relatively under control. Relatively enduring beliefs and values. Regains balance when shaken by external influences.
Absolutely Stable	Well-defined mindset to the point of rigidity. Emotional stoic to the point of frigidity. Impervious to external influences.
Dynamic	Well-defined mindset and emotions yet neither rigid nor frigid. Resilient to external influences. Adaptation displayed whenever required. Clear on when and how to respond to outside influences.

A stanza from the Bhagavad Gita explains this wonderfully:

Yogasthah kuru karmani
Sangam tyaktva dhananjaya
Siddhy–asidhyoh sama bhutva
Samatvam yoga ucyate

Unperturbed sameness in all conditions is 'yoga'. Engage therefore in actions steeped in yoga.

Type of Equilibrium	*Organizational Characteristics*
Unstable or Restless	Unclear or present prospects and uncertain about the future Fluid vision, mission and objectives Policies and procedures conflict each other and are not in alignment with core organizational purpose Morale of employees is low
Stable yet Imperfect	Present and future clearly articulated. Vision, mission and objectives laid down in simple and discernible way Policies and procedures are generally systematic. Morale of employees is conducive Tends to be off balance by external influences at times but is back to tract in general.
Absolutely Stable	Present and future too rigidly defined leaving no scope for adaptations or change. Vision, mission and objectives are preset and sacrosanct. Impervious to outside influences and therefore too inward looking.
Dynamic	Well-defined strategy for present and future, yet scope for adaptation, and change is inbuilt. Vision and mission are fixed yet immediate goals and tasks change in response to changes in external and internal environment.

There is a story told about the Zen Master Hakuin who lived in the Shien-Ji monastery. People in the nearby towns respected and revered him a lot. Near the monastery lived a family of merchants. One day the merchant and his wife discovered that their daughter was pregnant. On enquiry she named Hakuin as the father. The parents confronted Hakuin in great anger and verbally abused him in front of all his disciplines. 'Is that so?' was all what Hakuin said. Months later a baby boy was born and was given to the Zen master's care. By then, he had lost his reputation and many disciplines left him. Hakuin went about his life as before. He took care of the boy lovingly. A year later, boy's mother confessed truth to the parents that the real father of the boy was not Hakuin but a young man who worked on a farm elsewhere in the town. The father and mother went to Hakuin once again and apologized. They narrated the entire story to him. While giving away the boy to the couple in the same loving manner, he said with the same equanimity 'Is that so?'

LAW OF CYBERNETICS

Every complex system is made up of sub-systems which have their own adaptive relationship to each other and the system as a whole.
A control and communication process operates in the system and its parts that keeps it at a self-regulatory equilibrium.

LE CHÂTELIER'S PRINCIPLE

If a system in equilibrium is disturbed by changes in determining factors,
the system will tend to shift its equilibrium so as to counteract the effect of the disturbance.

AT A RUDIMENTARY LEVEL, EQUILIBRIUM DOES EXIST in individuals who go about their daily life normally and organizations that are ongoing concerns. If not, the individual would be mentally and emotionally unstable to conduct himself or herself in everyday life as we know it and an organization would have long ceased to exist.

In a state of dynamic equilibrium, the mind adapts itself so as to avoid destabilizing impact or at least return to its original state countering the effect of such an impact. The mind shifts temporarily its centre of gravity in such a way that the external force does not permanently throw it off balance. You must willfully assist this natural propensity of the mind by:

(i) perceiving facts beneath facades and intentions beneath actions.

(ii) discrimination between the essentials in life from non-essentials and elimination of the latter.

(iii) aligning your primordial state of being which is naturally at equilibrium.

Thus is equilibrium restored at a personal level even if disturbed by external events.

A mind in a state of dynamic equilibrium is like a majestic eagle encircling the skies far above, darting like an arrow. Yet it is itself unmoved and still. There is extreme movement as the wind brushes through its feathers. Yet there is utter stillness within. The eagle in its stillness observes every minute detail of the contours of the earth below. Nothing escapes its alert and watchful eyes. As it is with the eagle in flight so is it with the mind in state of dynamic equilibrium.

Such a mind passes through highly difficult and stressful situations, and yet is in itself neither at any difficulty nor at distress. The mind, purged of all its distorting adjuncts, flows in its primordial and natural course. It begins to see things as they are beyond what they appear to be.

A mind in a state of dynamic equilibrium is the repository of equanimity of the soul. A disturbed and fickle mind produces actions that are likewise. Equanimity is not a state of being unconcernd about the world but it is one of profound empathy unconditioned by personal bias or social prejudice.

The Buddhist text Dharmapada calls such a state of mind *upekkha* which literally means 'to patiently perceive'. You are in such a state in spite of 'standing in the middle of chaos' (Tatra-Majjhattata). Greek philosophers called it 'Ataraxia', mental detachment in the midst of activity.

6

Skill in Action

From Thinking in Real-Time to the Action Paradigm

PRINCIPLE OF WORK AND THE GIBBS FUNCTION

Work is the product of force and the distance over which it moves.
Gibbs function is the measure of the ability of a system to perform useful work.
It is the objective measure of the energy available in a closed system to perform useful work based on observation of the required active energy not available to do so.

IMPULSE MUST BECOME TEMPERED IN BEHAVIOUR AND motion must take the form of momentum. Then the work done will take the form of intelligible, meaningful and purposive action. This is skill in action. The energy expended by a leader will then create an ability on the part of his or her teammates to do useful work. Action originates in the mind, since action is behaviour with a qualitative meaning attached to it. The ability of the mind to spawn such action in turn depends on being clear-minded, right-minded and lofty-minded. For such is the mind of the best among scientists too. Work then produces the desired results. If not the energy employed and the effects produced will be futile.

Clarity comes from an understanding that grasps the core of each thing, its locus in the order of things and its structural make-up. Probe into the core of an idea or thought. Separate impressions from ideas. Be not a hasty prey to first impressions. Shun petty things and irrelevant details. A seer once said, 'Isolate the grains of truth from the chaff of fancies.' Get real. Let not your imagination turn to unfounded fancies. He clearly and rightly understands, who knows both knowledge and ignorance. Science after all is a journey that begins with ignorance and progresses on the path of factuality. As is it with science, so is it with life.

Being right-minded is a step above being clear-minded. A thing my be clearly plausible, but is it the right thing? Concealed trivialities can make the most credible into the blatantly implausible and impossible. Right thinking prepares the mind for any eventuality and as it is said, chance favours the prepared mind. Acknowledge every experience. Inspect carefully and decide which of those you will allow to influence you. In the race-cum-rally called life you must be wary of the opinions of others and those of your own. Beware of your mind's tendency to pre-judge. Let your mind not speculate beyond the confines of facts and reason. Let it not conjure things that are not. A decision based on conjectures is like an edifice built on twigs. The difference between the good and the bad, the beautiful and the ugly is one of degree only. The eye of reason sees the shades of grey in between the black and white, for, the opposite of a profound truth may well be another profound truth.

Being lofty-minded is an intensely personal affair. For those with power to guide the destinies of others, it becomes inescapably public responsibility too. Being high-minded is a step above being right-minded. It encompasses and goes beyond clear and right thinking. High mindedness is closely coupled with ethics, vision and one's lifetime purpose.

Don't let your reverence to reason walk on the ramp for applause from the onlookers. The applause will naturally follow if you respect and keep it private. Oppenheimer, the father of the atomic bomb that ended the bloody World War II, was a melancholic man after his rigorous effort succeeded and won him historic fame. He reluctantly developed the bomb that destroyed two thriving cities in Japan only to end further bloodshed. Yet, he was also the first to vociferously speak out against further research on the atom as part of war efforts.

Action is also a means of self-actualization. This does not mean you can do whatever you like to do always. At times compulsions and circumstances beyond your control will make you act in a way not exactly to your liking. Maybe what you do for your livelihood may not exactly be what you wish to do in life. If so, don't force yourself to either like or dislike what you do for a living. In it do make room for what you really are passionate about in life. Life and livelihood will then blend seamlessly. For, livelihood is an adjunct of life and not life itself. The designs of a boat vary, yet the 'boat' itself does not. For want of a different design, it is only a fool who will scuttle and sink the boat itself and himself too with it.

Gregor Mendel was a monk by profession, and a busy one at that with a lot of religious and ritualistic responsibilities. He still made enough room and time to pursue his personal passion of studying genetics and experimenting with pea plants in the monastery's garden. Mendel became the father of modern genetics. John Maxwell Coetzee was a computer programmer with IBM. He continued to nurture his passionate interest in life too. He wrote. Coetzee won the 2003 Nobel Prize for literature.

Once you are sufficiently capable and confident of your passion becoming a livelihood, take the plunge. I am sure Coetzee is no more sitting in a cubicle writing computer codes today.

LAW OF CONSERVATION OF ENERGY

Energy can neither be created nor destroyed; it can only be transformed from one form to another.
The sum of all energies in the system is a constant.
Mass can be converted to equal amount of energy and vice-versa.

NOETHER'S THEOREM

To every differentiable symmetry in action of a system or an entity there is a corresponding conservation law.

ACTION WITHOUT A PURPOSE OR MEANING IS ONLY A psychosomatic exertion. Exertion of the mind and body in such cases leads to a loss of energy and as an inevitable adjunct, time too. Energy is everywhere. Animate and inanimate objects are made up of matter. Matter is made up of atoms. Atoms are made up of electrons, protons and a nucleus. Still deeper within, the sub-atomic particle is simply a bundle of energy. You are thus a bundle of energy – cosmic and ethereal. As you move along in life you indulge in actions. Actions transform the self from one energy level into another. The cosmic energy of which you are a part is constant, even as it fluctuates, never losing or gaining in quantum. You only squander that which is yours in the cosmic whole of abundance by not transforming and using it for the right outcomes.

The fundamental theme of conservation is that an entity remains unchanged despite transformation of its secondary manifestations that are transient. A mythical world where anything can happen at any time is not real but fantastical. This is the world of imagination without restrictive rules. You can imagine that you have the body of Arnold Schwarzenegger, the money of Bill Gates, the brain of Einstein and the fame of Elvis Presley. Or it could be a combination of Marilyn Monroe, Paris Hilton and Madame Curie. The energy of the mind in wasted is such wishful pursuits. On the other hand, the Wright Brothers too imagined about human flight. They were passionate and rational. They believed with their heart and researched with rigorous reason. The unbound creative energy transformed itself into the realm of matter where energy is conserved. The result was human flight – the airplane. Conserve your energy and do not labour your mind and body in vain, for petty gains.

The Concept of 'Concorde fallacy' is very relevant here. The term relates to the supersonic Concorde project in the 1960s. British and French governments continued to fund the project despite knowing that it would never yield profits. There were a number of problems of time and cost overruns. Still the funding kept going with the logic that since so much has been invested already, a little more would not matter. The Concorde fallacy is, therefore, also known as the fallacy of sunk costs.

Another classic case of the Concorde fallacy was Sony's Betamax Video Recorders. Sony was the first to bring such a product in 1975. Within a year Sony's rival JVC brought out the VHS (Video Home System). Very soon there were many more Japanese companies making the same product. The management of Sony was unwilling to license Betamax Technology, whereas JVC was happy to share their VHS format. Since the two formats were incompatible, consumers were forced to decide between them. Towards the early 1980 Betamax-based machines were rapidly losing favour in the market. Sony still kept pumping money into Betamax VCRs. There were many technical problems too. Added to this there was intense price war. The leadership of Sony nevertheless lingered on with Betamax. It was only as recently as the year 2002 that Sony finally announced that it would be discontinuing Betamax products.

There was massive dislike in the US against its soldiers languishing in Vietnam. As the war progressed, casualties mounted rapidly. One study estimated the life expectancy of a US soldier in Vietnam was just 17 minutes. However, the US government and its leadership kept sending in more soldiers despite huge public protests. The logic was that since so many soldiers were already sacrificed it was a 'debt' to them that more soldiers would go and win the war – the Concorde fallacy again. How does one avoid it? By right perception and right knowledge.

In Indian epistemology the *pramana* is known as source of valid knowledge. Most schools of Indian epistemology believe in certain established *pramanas*, the primary ones being *pratyaksha, anumana, upamana* and *agama*.

Prakyatsha is knowledge gained by sense perception. Perception arises by contact of the senses and an object. *Anumana* is knowledge gained by inference. *Upamana* is knowledge gained by analogy and comparison. *Agama* is regarded by all the schools of philosophy and Vedanta 'as' a very important source of authentic knowledge. Agama also is known *sabdhapramana*. Its source is authoritative texts and the words and writings of men and women of wisdom. While all other sources of knowledge are subject to internal and external contradictions, *sabdhapramana* is regarded as inherently true and authentic.

All the sources of knowledge are subject to both reflection and refraction of truth since there is always a medium through which knowledge or truth is obtained. The belief in *agama*, the words of others, depends on the authenticity and trustworthiness of the individual who is its source.

With reflection and refraction comes clear thinking, with clear thinking comes correct perception without pride or prejudice.

NEWTON'S FIRST LAW

A stationary object remains stationary and a moving object continues to move in a straight line unless an external force acts on the object.

NEWTON'S SECOND LAW

The force producing acceleration in an object is proportional to the product of the mass of the object and its acceleration.

IF YOU THINK INERTIA IN YOUR PERSONAL AND professional life is an outcome of things being stationary and still, do think again. Paradoxically, you may well be in a state of inertia or stagnancy even as your life may appear to be on a roll.

Things are destined to remain as they are unless you act upon their destiny. Thus do you alter your own destiny as well. Freewill can be turned to willpower, one of the most potent of all transformative leadership powers. Like a timeless screenplay, it can beautifully script your destiny too.

All things in life are either still or in motion. All events move at a different pace in different time frames. There is change of varied degrees. The power that prompts things and events to remain as they are or to change is one and the same. The power to initiate movement where there is none or to halt the moment of an event for good or redirect it into a desirable direction is a power vested in you.

The role of a leader here can be likened to the captain of a ship who determines its speed and direction. He may speed up, slow down, change direction and take a detour or surge straight or full stream depending on the weather, intervening obstacles and contingencies. The decisions of a leader likewise determine the movement of the organization itself, and such decisions are at times unconventional. Let's take the case of Andy Grove, the CEO of Intel.

In the late 1970s, competition in the memory chip market was fierce. During the early 1980s Japan started producing memory chips of superior quality at lower cost. Andy Grove had a conversation with his colleague and co-founder of Intel Gordon Moore. 'What if the board kicked us out and a new CEO comes in? What would he do?' he asked Moore. 'He would get us out of memories,' Moore replied. 'Then let's walk out of the door, come back and do it ourselves' Grove said. From then on Intel moved on from memory chips to microprocessors. That was a defining movement in the lives of both Grove and Moore and in the history of Intel.

The results of a decision depend on the nature and quality of force with which it is translated into action. You may have the power, but do you have the force inherent in it to enable it to achieve your ends? Newton's second law has a precise answer to this question. Power is of many sources. It may arise out of your position, what you possess in general or a particular situation and so on.

But power in itself is at best a decorative appendage in life. Force must be innate in power for acts of power to be forceful. Forceful power propels or accelerates an event or individual to act at a pace that is desirable to achieve your intended objective.

The more powerful a situation or a person is to your detriment, the more tactfully forceful must the enactment of your power be. Though you may be relatively less powerful than that situation or person, the pace or acceleration with which you act or induce action will do the job for you.

Power is also the power to break barriers that confine imagination within narrow walls. An incident that turned out to be a defining moment for Andy Grove and Moore, the stalwarts, will exemplify this.

In 1994 Intel scientists discovered that its Pentium processor chip 'could' develop a minor error once in 27,000 years. This was hypothetical. IBM who was a major user of the chip considered stopping its inward shipment. Intel faced a serious credibility threat.

Andy Grove, the CEO of Intel had two choices – (a) reassure the world that the chip was good and fine since the likely fault was only a conjecture and that too could occur once in 27,000 years. (b) Replace each and every chip that was already with the customers at the cost of nearly half a billion dollars. Worst still this would stall or even abruptly halt the phenomenal growth the company was going through thereby letting its increasingly aggressive rivals take a lead.

Andy Grove did what rudimentary common sense would forbid. He recalled every chip and replaced each of them with a new one. He stopped the company that was racing at the pace of a rocket right in its tracks, or rather 'paused' it. Only to make it take off again with double the speed and confidence.

Forcefulness must at times be accompanied by swiftness and concreteness too. The Blitzkrieg strategy of attack in battles depends on swift and focused strikes by a less powerful entity over a stronger rival. This was employed successfully by legendary generals such as Romel of Germany and Patton of the United States.

Power is also directly proportional to the perceiver of it. The *perception* of power as such is more important than the *actual* power itself. Military deterrence between the Soviet Union and the USA during the cold wars and economic deterrence today between groups of nations are an example to this.

The awesome and symbolic military outfit of the Roman legions with the phylum, plumes and shield is a visual display of power which would unleash a destructive force. A man in blood-drenched white robes carrying a cross with a poignant smile amid menacing legionaries is more so a display of a far higher and nobler power. It accelerates at a pace incalculable by throught and reaches the hearts of the vast multitude. Every leader must ponder upon and introspect this.

The strategy of deterrence is widely followed in war. It gained prominence in the Cold War era. A number of tactics such as the containment, proxy wars, appeasement, etc. formed part of deterrence strategy. Deterrence is applicable in business and in personal relationship too. It thus confirms a part of provisional and personal relationship in business of existing companies to discourage potential entrants into their market by various methods. Creating barriers to entry and hostile takeovers form part of deterrence. At times strategic deterrence can be overtly ruthless. When James Brooke took over as CEO of Johnson and Johnson, his biggest challenge was at Tylenol, a painkiller. It was marketed as a high-priced drug and a market leader. But it was under attack by Bristol-Myers, which introduced a rival product Datrin. It began advertising Datrin as having the same ingredients as Tylenol but being much cheaper. James Brooke acted instantly. Even before Datrin was launched, it gave advertisements in leading newspapers that it was cutting the cost of Tylenol and began rolling out discounts to its retailers to immediately implement the same. He further used the goodwill of Johnson and Johnson to convince leading newspapers not to carry 'false' advertisements of its rival Bristol-Meyers.

In the animal world, such deterrence take on the appearance of poisonous ones to deter predator. Certain spiders behave like poisonous ants. Some species of wasps take on the colour of their poisonous counterparts of another specious.

But beware when you use the power and force without judgement and discretion, for Newton's third law as discussed in Chapter 1 is verily ever in operation in the world you live in, if not in the world thereafter.

LAW OF CONSTANT COMPOSITION

A given compound always contains some proportions by mass of its constituent elements. In other words, the relative amount of each element in a particular compound is always the same regardless of the source or preparation. Yet, a catalyst induces changes in the set of similar elements.

THE CAS, M.TECHS AND MBAS WILL ALWAYS BE THE SAME and even from the same 'source', i.e. institute, professional body, academy, etc. What makes the difference is what the leader does on them, with them and through them. As a leader, you must play the role of a 'catalyst' that induces a different end product with constituents of a given situation being the same. The same with the involvement of the leaders produces the difference. To some, this may sound metaphysical and philosophic. A few examples will make it sound utterly practical and pragmatic.

People in an organization may be the very ordinary and standardized in all respects. Yet the leader makes them do extraordinary things that will radically transform them and the organization. The leader recognizes their individual traits and grooms them. To put it in the form of an axiom, the quality of leadership alone can revive and rejuvenate Carlos Ghosn and Ranjana Kumar are two vivid examples of such near miracles.

Talent is often tacit and dormant. Yet it is a formidable force. The Indian Bank had an illustrious beginning. It was established on August 15th 1907 to serve the nation as part of the Swadeshi movement. By the 1990s, it came to symbolize all that was wrong with banks in the public sector of India. It had no net worth, a mountain of loans to recover and an army of rogue defaulters. The morale of its employees was at its nadir. Indiscriminate lending practices, archaic internal procedures and poor corporate governance was writ large all over it.

Enter Ms Ranjana Kumar, India's first women to head a public sector bank. She took the job no one wanted. In fact, the Indian Bank was headless for some time until Ranjana Kumar took over its reins in the year 2000. Reviving the sick and dying bank was a challenge that Ranjana Kumar took in the right earnest. What she achieved was a fantastic tale of success. She turned around the bank with a series of innovative measures and internal restructuring.

The bank declared its first dividend in 10 years in the year 2006. Here is the best part. Unlike Jack Welch of GE, she did not shut down ailing units or retrench employees. She achieved what was pronounced by financial pundits as the impossible. She did it with the very same employees and the very same unions with a so-called bureaucratic mindset in a bureaucratic set up. She woke them up from their morose slumber, enthused them and filled them with hope and courage. Above all, she made the future of the company their personal responsibility. While all her predecessors failed, she achieved the unthinkable with the same team of people.

The story of Nissan's turnaround by Carlos Ghosn is another apt example in this context. The behemoth automaker Nissan of Japan was once near bankrupt. Gohsn was named its CEO in June 2001 with an impossible mandate to turn it around. Business analysts wagered that he would certainly fail. Nissan was beyond redemption. But Ghosn did the apparently impossible and Nissan was back on its feet again sprinting ahead without a care. One of the first things he did after joining Nissan was to go on a tour to all its factories and offices and meet with the employees. The employees were of both Japanese and European origin. While official communication between them was not a problem, Ghosn wanted a qualitative shift in the way people of the two ethnic origins interacted. He published and distributed a small pocket-sized bilingual dictionary. This dictionary had words like 'team work', 'togetherness', 'achievement', 'goals', 'values' in both English and in Japanese. Ghosn achieved phenomenal success with the same employees, and in fact *through* them.

Great leaders are like seers. They have the attitude of 'renunciation' about their material success and attributing it to the efforts of their followers instead.

Reading Siddhartha's story fixed firmly in my mind
the idea that this capacity for renunciation
in the pursuit of exalted aims
is the very essence of human greatness.

— Sir C.V. Raman

FARADAY'S LAW OF ELECTROLYSIS

The amount of any substance liberated or deposited in electrolysis is proportional to the quantity of electrical energy. Electrolysis is a method of breaking chemically bonded elements and compounds by passing electric current through them.

A LEADER GENERALLY 'BUILDS'. HE IS AT ONCE BOTH AN architect who plans and a mason who with his dexterity binds the team and builds the organization. However there are times when a leader must not only build but also 'break' and 'separate'. He must break the rigid mindsets of his teammates and annihilate the barrier to new learning and flow of new ideas. A leader must at times 'shock' and jolt the team or the system at times. He must separate the best and the worst of the past and that of the present too. Only then can he envision the future and design and build the new. He must look back in order to see further ahead than the others. He must look below in order to see farther above than the others. He must also at times break into parts the 'here and now' within the present, for every 'present' has at both its ends the past and the future pulling in the opposite directions.

A leader must not only build bonds but at times break redundant and virulent ones too. The famous rock group The Beatles began as a regular band of the 1960s playing rock and roll. Later, they began experimenting with new genres. This skyrocketed them to super stardom. As mentioned earlier, Ranjana Kumar took over the reins of the ailing Indian Bank and turned it around to a highly profitable entity. This spectacular story is a case study in many business schools. Ranjana Kumar accomplished this daunting task by first studying the 'anatomy and physiology' of the ailing bank and then diagnosing the problems correctly. She weeded out the archaic systems, procedures and processes while retaining what was good in them.

One of the audacious things she did was to restructure the hierarchy of the monolithic public sector bank. This led to a shift from mindless bureaucracy to resilient business sense among its employees.

Let met cite another case: that of Om Prakash Butt and the government behemoth State Bank of India (SBI). Remember, we are talking of public sector undertakings which are known for their red tape and rigid processes, not just in India but the world over. The businessmen of the year award of 2008 were a contest of sorts. Tough decisions had to be made by the jury. The contestants included the likes of Mukesh Ambani, Chairman, Reliance Industries, Anil Ambani, Chairman, Reliance Group, the flamboyant and aviation baron Vijay Mallya, the ubiquitous Sunil Bharti Mittal of the giant telco Airtel and Kumar Mangalam Birla, who globalized his company. The name Om Prakash Butt, the Chairman of SBI, figured nowhere in terms of glamour and flashiness. But the award is based on something more tangible and profound than glamour.

Om Prakash Butt was overwhelmingly voted as the businessman of the year. He joined the State Bank of India in the year 1972 and grew up the ladder by dint of his hard work and innovativeness. In 2006 he became the Chairman of the largest bank in India. When he took over, the status of the bank was at its lowest ebb. While the private sector banks were surging ahead, State Bank of India was plummeting. Once upon a time the bank was a class apart from the rest and was in the exalted position of an advisory to the banks and the industry. Almost all policy decisions pertaining to revenue and finance were taken only in consultation with it. However, Om Prakash Butt witnessed his bank losing its preeminent position.

Changing the mindset and culture of the bank was therefore, his topmost priority when he took over as its Chairman. He launched a highly innovative programme called *parivartan* which was aimed at gathering feedback from every SBI employee in the world. But also personally sat down with SBI's top managers numbering about two thousand and asked them for suggestions to turn around the bank. He gathered ideas from management consultants, leadership Gurus and even spiritual and religious leaders. He took 20 top executives on a 5-day retreat which was also meant as a brainstorming vacation.

Mahatma Gandhi said 'Be the change you want to see in the world.' By being the change, he brought about and inspired change. The employees of SBI became more than just employees. They became responsible citizens of the bank. The citizen SBI experiment was a grand success and the public perception of the bank changed dramatically. Another innovative breakthrough was the tree of fulfilment that each employee had to fill up. Employees began to introspect and clarify their own needs and inner aspirations. From tellers and clerks to top executives, the citizens of SBI began to respond to customers with a higher degree of purpose and responsibility. A near miraculous turnaround was achieved.

HUYGENS' WAVE THEORY

The speed of light in denser medium is less than that in rarer medium.

AS DISCUSSED EARLIER, LEADERSHIP IS AN INHERENTLY personal and subjective thing yet it is also intensely objective and outward oriented. The medium through which the path-illuminating energy travels to its intended destination, or minds and hearts of others, does play a role in determining the relative time it takes to achieve its intended effect.

The *medium* is therefore the *means* by which the leader reaches out to the others.

In a highly structured and rigid organizational set up, a 'mechanistic' type of bonding exists between people. Rigidly defined bureaucratic channels of communication hinder quick communication of the path-illuminating energy. The hierarchical nature of the roles and role relationships tend to slow the flow even further. At times the message or vision that the leaders intend to communicate may also get blurred or distorted.

In a situation where the individuals to be guided are of a solid-state mindset, the task of the leader is rendered even more daunting. Emotional and attitudinal proximity to good and positive-minded people will result in a transference of their positive energy to you. The Saint Poet Vemana puts this lucidly as follows: 'By long pilgrimage and visiting holy shrines the spiritual gains you obtain, can verily be gained if you seek the company of saints. Sacred is the water where a river meets the ocean, O child of the benevolent Vema, Listen.'

This is equally true in the mundane and material sense too. All humans are vulnerable to the psychological fact of 'self-fulfilling prophesy'. You are what you think and believe to be. What you think and believe to be is largely an outcome of the people in whose midst you spend your time. The power of the peer group in influencing your personality is not limited to childhood or teenage alone. It is a lifelong thing. The company you keep and the people to whom you are close will determine your character to a large extent. As is the character, so is the will, as is the will, so are the thoughts, and as are thoughts so is the way you conduct yourself in life.

The self-fulfilling prophecy is very real. In India elders tell their children not to utter negative words or nurture negative thoughts because there are 'devas' (gods) who say *thathastu* (so be it). Positive thoughts result in positive words and actions. Self-fulfilling prophecy is the power to alter actions in a positive manner and therefore, ensuring that the results of such actions are also positive and good. Research of self-hypnosis and auto-suggestions also prove this fact. Phrases like 'Today is going to be a good day', 'I am going to he happy today', 'I will not lose my temper today come what may', etc., in the morning are bound to have an effect likewise on you.

The influence that can be exerted between people need not be limited to a member relying on intellectual endeavour. Albert Einstein for instance while recounting his discovery of the special theory of relativity would explain how he was influenced by the philosophic metaphysical writings of David Hume and Mach.

The influence a person has on another or on others need not necessarily stem out of physical proximity. It can be remote influence from far away or from another time period. Mahatma Gandhi was very much influenced by John Ruskin's work *Unto This Last*. Gandhiji decided at once to change his own life and went on to publish his own newspaper *Indian Opinion* in South Africa. He set up the Phoenix Settlement in South Africa where people lived and worked without distinction of race, nationality or creed. Gandhiji also translated *Unto This Last* into Gujarati in 1908.

Immanuel Kant, the famous German thinker, called this the 'Categorical Imperative'. The *Bhagavad Gita* captures its essence in simpler terms:

yad yad ācarati śreṣṭhas
tat tad evetaro janaḥ
sa yat pramāṇaṁ kurute
lokas tad anuvartate

'Whatever action a great man performs, common men follow. And whatever standards he sets by exemplary acts, all the world pursues'.

There are three classes of people:
those who see,
those who see when they are shown,
those who do not see.

— Leonardo da Vinci

PRINCIPLE OF REACTION AND ITS TYPES

A reaction is a mutual action of chemicals on each other or on some form of energy such as heat, light, electricity resulting in a change in one more of these agents.
In an exothermic reaction, heat energy is released.
In an endothermic reaction, heat energy is absorbed.
In a homogeneous reaction, all reactors are in the same physical state. In a heterogeneous reaction all reactants are in different physical states.

REDOX REACTION

A reaction in which transfer of electrons takes place from one reactant to another reactant.

OXIDATION REACTION

It is a reaction and a process involving loss of electrons. This results in an increase in positive charge or decrease in negative charge.

REDUCTION REACTION

It is a process which involves gain of electrons. There will be a decrease in positive charge or an increase in negative charge.

A REACTION IS ANY ACTION THAT RESISTS ANOTHER action or force acting upon it. It is a movement in the contrary direction of a force or form of energy. It is a counter to an existing tendency. A reaction is often born out of anger and its conjoined twins – haste and hubris. The three have led to phenomenal leadership failures the history. Many powerful and kings emperors have perished due to decisions made in anger, haste or hubris. Empires have disintegrated and so have organizations because of some decisions and acts of their leaders. Even the most successful of leaders must be wary of this at both personal and professional levels. For at stake are one's career and character at one end and the company at the other.

Roberto Goizueta, the CEO of Coca Cola, was acknowledged as cool-headed leader and a marketing genius. Yet, his rival Pepsi was fast eating into Coke's market share. Goizueta reacted hastily with his Pepsi challenge campaign and brought out the New Coke in 1985. He changed the nearly 100-years-old formula based on taste tests. This is regarded as one of the greatest blunders in managerial decision making. The New Coke was an utter disaster. The old formula had to be brought back.

The world's richest man could have been one Gary Kildall and not Bill Gates had it not been for a short but impulsive burst of irritation on the former's part. When in 1980 a team of blue-suited IBM executives knocked his door, it was the knock of good fortune of mythical proportions. IBM had struck a deal with Bill Gates for providing programming software for its PCs. Gates however did not have an operating system and referred

IBM to Kildall. Gates knew that Kildall had invented the CP/M operating system. IBM desperately wanted to launch its own version of an operating system to counter the phenomenal popularity of the Apple II Computer. Kildall had to simply sign on the dotted line to fame, success and of course, a huge mountain of money. But why in the heavens did he not? Because he and his wife were irritated and upset over the thick non-disclosure agreement that the blue-suited IBM executives had brought with them. Bill Gates stepped in. He bought the QDOS from a small downtown firm, tweaked it and sold it to IBM as MS-DOS. The rest is history. As for the past, well, hindsight will never be pleasant for Gary Kildall at least.

You must usually 'respond' to situations, yet you must react at times when circumstances so demand. That reaction can be a façade or a concocted one for one reason or the other. In any case, the reaction must be fully within your will and control. The reaction must be driven by reason in its bridle and not unbridled emotions such as anger or wrath. A reaction is a vent to convey a particular idea, emotion or a message to others. A reaction of this kind is exothermic in nature. When you do so endothermically, the energy from outside is absorbed by you. In many cases, it is the negative energy that is absorbed. For, a leader like a sponge often absorbs and soaks up negativity of his teammates. In the exothermic reaction positive energy is strongly and spontaneously emitted out. In a reaction that is endothermic in nature negative or disruptive energy outside the self is absorbed and is drained of its virulent effects.

When the leader's reactive power is directed at those of his own kind in status or role it is a homogeneous reaction. When it is directed to those quite unlike, the reaction is heterogeneous. While indulging in the former, you may want to use the 'blowpipe' technique of the reactive process wherein your reaction is mediated by another person or object. In other words, you must display preparedness for the eventuality that there would be a counter-reaction. With the latter, the 'flame' technique works better. This reaction reveals the real colour or camouflaged nature of your teammates and rivals alike. The decrease in negativity and increase in overall positivity is as applicable to the organization as it is to the individual. The number of negative attitudes and traits tend to vary inversely with that of the positive within an individual. As discussed earlier, the individual is in a matrix of the three *doshas* and the three *gunas*. When say, *tamas* – the *guna* of ignorance and nescience – increases, the *satva* characterized by knowledge and purity is relatively reduced. The vice-versa is likewise true.

As it is with the individual so is it with an organization. The increase in negativity or negatively charged personalities has the effect of decreasing positivity and positively charged personalities. The converse is equally true. This fundamental principle of science evident all across the known universe was enshrined in the spiritual lore of different traditions. The *Bhagawat Gita* consists of many *slokas* testifying that the company of the good turns even the most wicked into the good. The Holy Bible and the Holy Granth Sahib and other holy texts also teach the same.

The number of positive thoughts you have in life at an individual level and the number of positively charged personalities you surround yourself with are vital for personal and organizational success.

The story of Joanne Kathleen Rowling (J.K. Rowling) is a sterling example of how the power of positive thought can help one surmount the most negative of circumstances. She worked as a secretary in a publishing firm where she was in charge of sending rejection slips. Perhaps, this was a prelude to what she herself would get in the years ahead until her breakthrough. She hit upon the idea of a boy wizard in 1990 during a train journey from Manchester to London. The idea would become a reality in the form of a book after seven long years of tears and turmoil. Meanwhile, her mother died of a prolonged illness. This loss compounded her troubles. As means to escape from her sorrow, Rowling accepted a teaching job and moved to Portugal. In 1992 she married a journalist but the marriage lasted only about a year. Rowling was now left to fend for herself and her baby girl named Jessica.

She returned to England with her daughter. Her personal life nose-dived. She lived in abject poverty in a tiny mice-infested flat even as she dealt with deprivation and suicidal tendencies. She sat in roadside cafes with her daughter sleeping by her side while she wrote her first book *Harry Potter and the Philosopher's Stone*. It is said that she manually wrote copies of the book to be sent to different publishers because she could not afford to make copies of the draft.

All leading publishers rejected the book. Children's book publishers Bloomsbury gave her the breakthrough. But they had two pieces of advice for her. The first was to get a day job because in their view there was not much money to be made in children's books. The second was to use her initials rather than her first name because they thought boys would be biased against reading a book written by a woman.

Today J.K. Rowling is one of the richest women on earth, and arguably the richest author ever.

In an interview with NBC's Katie Couric, Rowling narrates an incident that happened when she once passed by the tiny flat in which she had lived. She burst into tears on laying her eyes on it. At the window of the flat she could see herself standing and looking into the horizon. Amid tears, she consoles her own self standing at the window uttering words of confidence and declared with poignant confidence that one day this misery will end.

'...However much this hurricane whirled around me – I stayed true to what I wanted to write.' Rowling says in another interview. That's the power of positive thoughts and 'responding' to situations while not 'reacting' to them.

By responding to situations and keeping the reactionary impulses under check one can accept the opinion of others and evaluate them objectively. Such receptiveness to feedback is vital for personal and professional leadership. Here is when the laws of positive and negative feedback come into play, as will be seen in the following page.

CLAUDE BERNARD'S THEORY OF HOMEOSTASIS

It is the property of an open or closed systems to regulate its internal environment so as to maintain a stable, constant condition or homeostasic balance. Dynamic equilibrium adjustments and regulatory mechanisms make homeostasis possible.

Most homeostatic control systems require both positive and negative feedback mechanism.

POSITIVE FEEDBACK MECHANISM

These are designed to accelerate or enhance the output created by a stimulus that has already been activated. They push levels out of normal ranges.

They cascade the effect of the stimulus. Yet it is risky if the acceleration becomes uncontrollable.

NEGATIVE FEEDBACK MECHANISMS

They reduce or suppress the original stimulus. They keep conditions from exceeding tolerable limits.

The purpose is to prevent sudden changes, so radical and severe that they may result in the collapse of the entire system.

WITHIN AN ORGANIZATION, A LEADER MUST INSTITUTIONALIZE a feedback mechanism. The feedback can be both positive or negative. The former must be accepted but must not result in complacency. The latter must not be snuffed out nor must it result in fatalism or compromise.

'An unsatisfied customer is our most important resource', said Bill Gates, the co-founder of Microsoft. What he is talking of here is the need for receptiveness to negative feedback. An organization must be responsive to such feedback in order to be resilient to its own future. Negative feedback too has the power to initiate an introspective process both within an individual and an organization alike. Sharing ideas, exploring attitudes between individuals and divisions will enhance both individual and organizational performance. Though positive and negative feedback have different meanings and usage, they could be made to serve a common purpose – your personal and professional excellence and success.

In fact, there have been people who have consciously encouraged negative feedback. Henry Ford actually formalized a 'contention system' whereby top managers openly debate and argue against each other's ideas.

You, as a leader, must respond to negative feedback in certain ways as elucidated below:

Type of response	*Negative feedback is correct.*	*Negative feedback is incorrect.*
Confirmatory	Check veracity and accept it.	Check veracity and clarify if it's correct.
Corrective	Take steps to amend the situation.	Set right misconceptions. Eliminate the 'courses' that let one to form the feedback.
Explanatory	Explain to the team and make them understand the need to change.	Explain why it is incorrect to ensure it does not repeat.
Diagnostic	Analyze the situation and understand it.	Understand the reasons and circumstances that led to such a feedback. These may be hidden and chronic in nature.

A system, social or biological, is made of parts that interact with each other. In nature there is a well-established feedback system both in the animal and physical realms. Feedback is important for both the individual and the group. A good feedback system enables receipt of information that is qualitatively correct and optimal in time. Such a feedback guides actions to perform in the present with desired results in the future. Feedback influences both the quality and quantity of the output.

At an individual level a person must be open to receive feedback without misconceptions or prejudice. This makes communication process a continuous and also sustainable one. Communication by default assumes receipt of feedback. This is how new ideas evolve and new paradigms of action come into being.

The most important thing about feedback fulfilling its positive goodwill is the will and attitude of the receiver. There is an interesting Zen parable that will illustrate this. Once a learned man well versed in many scriptures and noble lineage approached a Zen monk in monastery. The Zen monk was very famous for his knowledge and wisdom. The learned man walked up to the monk who was sitting in a garden and expressed his desire to become his disciple. He went to explain his background and the vastness of his knowledge. The Zen monk shook his head and politely gestured the man to leave. Just then a simple looking farmer approached the monk and expressed his desire to join the monastery. The monk smiled and welcomed him.

The learned man who saw this was perplexed and asked him as to why he was not allowed while the farmer was allowed into the monastery. The monk asked one of his disciples to fetch him a cup filled to the brim with tea and a jar with more tea. He then asked the man to fill the cup. 'How can I?' asked the learned man, 'I see that it is already full, and therefore it will not accommodate any more tea.'

The monk smiled and said, 'Your mind too is like this cup that is already full. Empty your cup first and then you are welcome to join the monastery to learn.'

LAWS OF IMMUNOLOGY

Components of the immune system are not modular although most include some part architectural features like the single spleen, etc. The larger animal lives longer than a smaller one. Hence, the immune system has to do a better job in protecting it.

DINOSAURS WERE HUGE. THEY WERE THE FIRST TO PERISH when the ice age began. Many smaller species of that age like the Tuatara still survive today. If you think just size is all that matters to survive or win, think again. Your biggest strength could turn out to be your most formidable weakness in certain situations. Your ability could turn out to be your debility.

In 1917, Bertie Charles Forbes compiled his first list of 100 largest American companies. In 1987, *Forbes* magazine republished its original 'Forbes 100' list. When compared with its 1987 list, 61 companies of the original group had ceased to exist! Of the remaining 39, only 18 managed to stay in the top 100.

I am tempted to quote a few lines from my book *The 7th Sense* in this context. It's a limerick at the beginning of chapter 1 of the book which captures the essence of defensive strategies and their relevance.

You may be the predator-king
But you are likewise the prey.
A watchful player you must be
In life's game where friends and foes are in the fray.
Then shall you triumph here and now today
Or live to win another day.

The five important issues to be considered in defence at personal and professional level are as follows:

1. Defend what is the really worth defending. Eliminate the chaff from the grain, stick to fundamentals.
2. Defend everything that is important with equal force. Pre-empt potential attacks and make appropriate preparations.
3. Understand your attacker or competitor and assess his strengths and weaknesses.

Defence can be done in poise and with etiquette in such away that it might not overtly be defensive.

There are many types of defensive strategies. Fortified defence involves barricading yourself against attacks. This involves strengthening yourself within and making it a deterrent against potential attackers or competitors. In business this includes efforts to enhance customer loyalty and brand equity.

Model defence involves a more dynamic and flexible response. This involves making it hard for the attacker or competitor to locate your strengths and weaknesses thereby the rival is ill informed about your strategies. A good leader employs both these defensive strategies effortlessly and often simultaneously. A quality that is very important for defending one's position is 'patience'. It will always take time to dissuade the attacker or persuade someone to accept ideas. Be open to arguments and counter-arguments. Refine those of yours as you proceed.

7

The Dream Team

On Building, Sustaining and Stewarding It

CONCEPT OF CURVED SPACE AND TIME

In flat space-time physical coordinates all forms of energy including light too travel parallel to each other. In curved space-time, two or more entities curve in alignment with a propensity to meet each other. Forms of energy that are apparently parallel and exclusive are in fact synergistic and inclusive.

SPACE IS OF DIFFERENT TYPES – OUTER (THE WORLD OUT there containing people and things) and inner (the world within which impressions of the world keep fleeting past, some enduring longer than the others). As mentioned earlier, matter is itself ultimately energy. Energy of the self can change 'space' – the tapestry on which daily events transpire, – and 'time' – the duration within which they occur.

Thus, all that happens and where, how and when they happen can be influenced by energy that is within you and energy that is in fact you. There is synergy when two like-minded people with similar nature and levels of energies team up. Their attitudes and views are parallel and do not dissect. But there is at times even greater synergy when people unlike join together. Their interaction in the space–time continuum is not parallel but curved. At the point where the energies 'blend' to reach out and meet each other, there is stupendous success. The individuals thus influence and are influenced by each other. Like two pillars that hold up an edifice though being apart spatially, two or more unlike individuals make up for what each lacks and therefore function remarkably well for the common purpose.

There is much evidence to the magic that such combination can produce. Opposites when aligned in a certain manner, far from contradicting each other in fact, flawlessly compliment each other. The relative pace with which ideas and attitudes of one individual changes with respect to the other can benefit the individuals and the organization. This is evident in the transformational law of Lorentz that follows.

LORENTZ TRANSFORMATION

Measurement of space and time of two different observers differ where one observer is in constant motion with respect to the other.

NO TWO PEOPLE ARE INHERENTLY EXACTLY ALIKE. EVEN when predominantly similar, they may arrive at different judgements on perceived facts and events. This is because though similar, a subtle yet inexorable change is constantly occurring within each individual at ideational and emotional levels. There is a movement and metamorphosis within, the pace of which is highly personalized. Like the pinch of a pebble in one's shoe, it can be verbalized but the experience itself is unique to the individual. This in turn leads to differences in judgement. Thus while you may have to judge do not be judgemental. Do not shun difference.

As Donald Trump, the famous New York real-estate developer, said, 'You can't know it all. No matter how smart you are, no matter how comprehensive your education, no matter how wide-ranging your experience, there is simply no way to acquire all the wisdom you need to make your business thrive.'

Steve Ballmer, the Present CEO of Microsoft, met Bill Gates, the would-be founder of Microsoft, at Harvard University. Ballmer was interested in business, while Gates was enamoured with computer programming. By being different, they complimented each other. They became friends. Gates persuaded Ballmer to join Microsoft as its first business manager. At that time during the late 1970s Microsoft had only twenty three employees and its annual sales were meager. The rest is history, a living one at that.

This leadership energy gets uniformly and evenly spread out across the organization as we will see in the Ampere's circuital law that follows.

AMPÈRE'S CIRCUITAL LAW

Two parallel wires carrying magnetic currents in the same direction attract each other magnetically.

LORENTZ FORCE

It is the force exerted on a charged particle in an electromagnetic field.
The particle will experience a force due to electric field and magnetic field.

YOU CANNOT PLAY MENTOR TO EACH AND EVERY MEMBER of your team individually. More so, you cannot do it for an infinitely long period of time. In large teams continuous personal contact is neither feasible nor advisable. You must pass down your leadership magnetism to others, especially the next-rung teammates. You must build leaders. Your physical presence will then not be mandatory for the cohesiveness of the team. The members of the team attract each other and will function in harmony towards larger organizational purpose.

But having or grooming the right counterpart, be it a deputy or a partner, is a classic leadership trait that will be true for eternity. You must seek, obtain, nurture and be nurtured by a person who must be your 'alter-ego'. Even the most secluded of 'lone rangers' in history did have such a person. Akio Morita and Masaru Ibuka together turned a small radio repair shop in a bombed-out Tokyo building into one of the first truly global corporations called Sony. While Ibuka spawned technical innovations to new markets, Morita had the uncanny ability to study cultures of the East and West and blend the best parts of each into Sony's business strategy. During his later years he was often consulted on matters pertaining to US-Japanese trade issues.

William Proctor began his business as a candle maker. His father-in-law suggested that he team up with his brother-in-law James Gamble. Proctor found that Gamble's stability and organized approach counter-balanced his own creative spurt of ideas. The company then founded and set on a firm track in their very lifetimes was Proctor & Gamble.

BERNOULLI EQUATION

Sum of all forms of energy in a fluid flowing along a well-defined path (a streamline) is the same at any two points in that path.

WHEN A GATHERING OF INDIVIDUALS ARRIVES AT A common consensus and purpose, the gathering becomes a group with a common objective and shared means. When unified focus is achieved among all members, the group's actions too are focused though their personal views, maybe varied and different. The group thus becomes a team. When such a singular harmonious flow of purpose and focused action is established, the energy levels at all points in the organizational systems, sub-systems and functional areas is constant, regular and harmonious. The organization thus becomes 'boundaryless', to borrow a favourite phrase of Jack Welch (although he refers to it in a different context).

Kaizen, the unique structure of many Japanese organizations, refers to a 'headless' combine of teams. Hierarchy is minimal. Such an ideal organizational democracy is difficult to be translated into reality. Many have tried it and have not been quite successful. Breaking the hierarchy and control systems first in order to usher in Kaizen is like cutting your toes to fit into your shoes. Kaizen will evolve naturally and effortlessly on its own if individual energies in an organization flow seamlessly from conscious purpose to conscientious action.

The one who achieves this would be the loftiest among leaders. Such leaders may be senior in rank but do not consider themselves superior from even the employee performing a relatively trivial job. Yet, they are revered by all and their energy continues to flow evenly throughout the organization.

BERNOULLI PRINCIPLE

The decrease in the pressure of a free-flowing fluid as its speed increases is called Bernoulli Effect. This happens since ideal free-flowing fluids tend to conserve their energy.

A LEADER MUST CONSTANTLY INVOLVE HIMSELF IN THE organizational process and interact with those involved when the progress to the goal is in a nascent stage or if the people involved in it are new to the task. You must exert firm yet gentle pressure on them. The pressure must be conducive but not coercive. It must gently guide and not deride. Like the unseen hand of a divine being that guides innumerable streams into winding rivulets and the rivulets into a mighty river, the leader must chart out the path, both in its larger and finer contours, of his team and his organization.

Ambiguities and uncertainties that add to work pressure of the team and to individual stress will thus be evened out. The speed with which processes flow towards the collective goal will increase exponentially.

PERTURBATION THEORY

(Time Independent and Time Dependent)

By beginning with a simple sub-system, and creating a 'disturbance' (perturbation), ripples are created in related systems whose hidden qualities are revealed.

We thus slowly yet surely and systematically understand the complex whole.

A COMPLICATED SYSTEM OR SITUATION CAN BE UNDERSTOOD with reference to a simpler one. At the heart of complexity is simplicity. Things in life are essentially simple. The most profound truths are often the simplest. The mind posits complexity. For, the mind in delusion is at home with complexity. Forever creating and seeking to probe into it, it strives to escape from the fact that at its core everything is simple.

Complexity is a human creation. To understand at once the whole, begin by the simplest and most rudimentary of its parts. Stoop down; begin at the roots to understand the vast sprawling canopy of the tree. If you make haste to reign over the 'big' at once, you shall be lost in the labyrinth of complexity. Patiently probe into the 'small' and it shall lead to a slow yet certain understanding of the larger entity.

To grasp the beauty and contours of a pond, just drop a pebble at its centre and watch the ripples spread.

From a strategic viewpoint, creating a ripple or disturbance in a certain part of an unknown terrain will reveal the entire terrain. The flaws or weaknesses in a system will be exposed. By constantly creating a perturbation the roots of complexity are approached. At the roots, it's all rudimentary. The immensity of the tree that they nurture is at once revealed.

BOYLE'S LAW FOR A GAS

At constant temperature the volume of a confined ideal gas varies inversely with its pressure.

ONCE THE TEAM IS ENTHUSED INTO ACTION AND THE 'heat is on' so to say, the leader need not mount pressure on the team or on any of its members. The 'cybernetics' within the team will, even without the leader's intervention, bring it back to the desired state of activity level when disturbed. In fact, in such situations, pressure exerted on the team by the leader may actually have an inverse impact on the morale of the team. In extreme cases, the volume of a team's output in terms of their actions and results may in fact reduce.

Complete and absolute autonomy to the team is not advisable even if the team becomes a 'headless combine' with clear vision, objectives and activities. A reasonable degree of guidance is needed because even a loosely bound gaseous team is never ideal.

A good leader displays tolerance to deviations and to ambiguity. In a world that is moving at a fast pace, deviations in performance by your team and ambiguities presented by situations must be viewed with an extended degree of tolerance. You can thus set deviations in their proper direction again. You can thus infuse clarity in ambiguous situations by assessing them objectively.

MENDEL'S LAW OF DOMINANCE

In a cross between parents of pure yet
contrasting traits,
only one form of trait will appear in
the next generation.
Each hereditary characteristic is
controlled by two factors
or allies which separate and pass into separate
reproductive cells.

IDEAS AND EMOTIONS INSPIRE ACTION AND ARE LIKEWISE revealed in action. When an individual is subjected to two contrasting ideas that go into accomplishing a task, only one idea will dominate in determining his or her actions. And that idea is revealed in the action itself. Imperceptible and intangible ideas and emotions are made perceptible, tangible and are 'reproduced' through the acts they inspire.

Do not subject someone to two contrasting ideas of equal relevance with equal intensity. Though in theory this may seem to inspire introspection and profundity, in practice, it will only confuse the person. What follows such a decision made is such mental frame of mind that leads to ill-founded and chaotic action.

Appeal to the hearts and minds of people with thrilling and easily discernible examples and ideas when you speak to cause action. When you talk against global warming, do make sure that you conserve electricity and fuel in your home and office. Before you vociferously advocate corporate citizenship, do pay your personal taxes promptly. Do make all such acts known.

The leadership traits you pass on to your follower must not be at the cost of the latter losing such a trait that is born or acquired by his or her own self. The skills you intend to reproduce in a follower must be inclusive of the best of his or her own and not exclusive. Your energy must replenish and reinvigorate, not replace or relegate what is native to the follower. It must have a cumulative effect and not a curtailing one.

Mentoring, something which was a familiar practice in many professions in the ancient world, is finding its foothold again. What was a part of ancient cultures has reincarnated itself due to necessity. With competition it is imperative to have a workforce that is effective and quick to act. In the frenzied and increasingly depersonalized work environment today there is a greater need for people to form meaningful connections with others.

The engagement and retention of talent and transmission of leadership wisdom to successors is of critical importance today. A recent Hackett Best Practices Survey of 2000 global companies cited succession management and planning as the single most important challenge to a leader. In his autobiographical book "*Straight from the Gut*" Jack Welch talks of the seriousness with which his predecessor embarked on a long and gruelling task of choosing his successor. Welch too embarked upon a similar exercise to choose his successor, Jeff Immelt. Many doubted Immelt's ability to match Welch's charisma and audacity. Yet, here were the laws of Mendel at play.

Welch mentored Immelt and groomed him in his own likeness. Immelt had his own characteristic leadership traits. The two were synthesized when Immelt took over as CEO of GE from Jack Welch to produce a newer equally successful hybrid GE, so to say. In fact this was the case with Jack Welch himself and his predecessor-cum-mentor Reginald H. Jones.

Martha Stewart achieved phenomenal success with her flamboyance and entrepreneurial spirit. Her company

Omnimedia grew in leaps and bounds. Even as it evolved, Stewart retained it as a 'one-woman' control entity. She intervened in day-to-day working of the company, even to the extent of herself appearing in TV advertisements. When a major legal problem broke out and the share prices of her company fell, there was no one to handle it in the absence of the ubiquitous Stewart.

At times there may be an apparent break with the immediate past which may in fact be in continuity with the historic ethos of an organization. A classic case of this is that Louis Gerstner who is credited to have saved the behemoth IBM from going out of business in the early 1990s.

After becoming its unlikely CEO in 1993 (others who were considered for the job included the likes of Bill Gates and Jack Welch) this relative 'novice' reversed the strategy of his immediate predecessor John Akers. He resisted attempts to break down IBM into independent units and turned it into an information technology integrator. In his book *Who Says Elephants Can't Dance?* he describes how he remedied and 'cured' IBM's culture that had become 'Balkanized'.

From the evolution of the individual leader, we shall now move on to organizational evolution. Let's look at what the evolutionary laws of Lamarck and Hardy have to offer.

LAMARCK'S THEORY OF EVOLUTION

Functions create organs and heredity determines the change in future generations. Environmental changes generate new needs. These needs determine use or otherwise of some organs. Existing organs may thus diminish and new organs may develop.

These are acquired characteristics which become hereditary.

THE KIWI, NATIVE OF AUSTRALIA, IS A FLIGHTLESS BIRD. It was a high flyer once but its wings slowly degenerated because of disuse. The little finger on human feet was very prominent when once our ancestors used to indulge in a lot of climbing and even more swinging (over trees!) It will vanish as a vestigial organ one day in the future. The legs of today's amphibians were fins when they were once completely aquatic.

The systems and structure of an organization evolve in response to the external environment. This is not a dramatic change but a steady adaptation.

Only the fittest survive according to Darwin.

As is it with this primordial law of nature, so is it with organizations. The systems and structures will and must adapt to external changes. Yet, there can be continuity-in-charge. New sub-systems and sub-structures will evolve. However, there is and at times must be a connection with the old.

Even as non-similar traits are acquired and blend seamlessly in the process of leadership development, certain continuity with the past exists. As discussed elsewhere in this book in a different context, the old merges with the new and selective elements of it are retained. Let me cite an example from GE itself since it figured in the earlier pages (Ah! There is continuity here too).

Way back in 1894 Charles Coffin took over from the legendary Thomas Alva Edison as the CEO of General Electric (GE), a company that the latter had founded. While Edison was a creative genius and engineer, Coffin was a brilliant engineer of organizations. He restructured the fast growing company with specific product lines and role-relationships. He introduced sound financial control mechanisms and was able to consolidate GEs position.

Charles Swope who succeeded Coffin in 1922 took these positive organizational development initiatives further with his own tinge of employee-oriented measures. He introduced many schemes such as group insurance, profit sharing, bonuses, pensions, etc which earned him the loyalty of the employees and led to the further consolidation of GE's market position.

Then came the forced and unnatural clean break with the past in the form of Charles Wilson, who undid most of the established practices and organization development initiatives that had grown from the days of Coffin. For years thereafter, GE went through a major crisis in industrial relations.

Evolution is a continuous process, which must be allowed to take its course. Success that comes this way is more enduring, lasting and enjoyable. That which comes by shortcuts and the easy way will leave by shortcut even more easily.

The idea of HCL (Hindustan Computers Limited) was born in 1976 in a cafeteria of DCM Cloth Mills at Delhi. Shiv Nadar was among the handful of engineers who were discussing the need to set up their own venture. They quit and decided to set up a company that would make personal computers. The experience they had was only in DCM's Calculator Division and the start-up fund was also a problem. Shiv Nadar recollects that nevertheless they would hang out together, crib together, have fun and work together. They first started a company called Microcomp Limited that manufactured digital calculators. This gave them enough money to evolve into a company that could manufacture computers in India. Very soon HCL was established.

Around that time companies like IBM left India. This left a major vacuum that Shiv Nadar quickly turned into an opportunity. HCL was just two years behind its American counterpart Apple Computers in making micro computers. In the early 1980s Shiv Nadar led his team to indigenously developed Relational Database Management System (RDBMS) at par with global peers. Very soon Shiv Nadar set his sights beyond Indian borders. HCL's Singapore venture was a success. Now Shiv Nadar evolved HCL towards computerization rather than selling computers. He noticed that most banks in India were shifting to UNIX platform. With some re-engineering done on computers, Shiv Nadar's team brought out the Busybee, as a UNIX-based computer. By late 1980s HCL became one of the largest IT companies in India.

Shiv Nadar then made forays into the American computer hardware market. But the venture failed miserably. But this did not deter Shiv Nadar. As a true leader does, he evolved as a better person after the failure, and so did HCL. In 1997 HCL spun off HCL Technologies Limited and formally entered the global software market. From the 70s through the 90s the story of

HCL was that of continuity-in-change as it evolved. Shiv Nadar also initiated redesigning of HCL when he realized the revenue from hardware sector was shrinking. In 1999 Shiv Nadar decided that the time was right for entering into capital market. HCL's Initial Public Offer (IPO) was an instant success. We can thus see how the changes in the environment generate new needs and thus needs give rise to new structures (organs) in business. Lamarck's Theory of Evolution and continuity-in-change operates subtly but surely in realms of personal and professional leadership.

The state owned Telecommunications Behemoth Bharat Sanchar Nigam Limited (BSNL) is another example in this context. In the early 2000s it was among the top telecommunication companies and the largest in terms of the number of customers in India with a bouquet of service offerings. Less than a decade later, it became another 'IBM' of the mid-1980s surfeit with problems like unmanageable scale of operations, ruthless competition from more agile companies, dwindling revenues and severe cash crunch. Louis V. Gerstner took over the reins of IBM at that critical time and turned it around. This story which is a case of study in top management schools is narrated by Gerstner himself in his book 'Who says elephants can't dance'. In 2008 BSNL too launched such an ambitious transformational exercise titled 'Project Shikhar'.

This was aimed at articulating and implementing a clearly defined multi-pronged strategy for BSNL's revival. The bedrock of this project was a pan-organizational restructuring. From a traditional bureaucratic set-up where work was done in silos, a dynamic Business Unit (BU) based organization was up with clearly defined roles. The aim was to make BSNL more resilient to customer needs, more agile in decision making and quicker to respond to emerging market needs. BSNL is being geared up to the status of pro-active warrior in a sector marked with ruthless competition for customers and tariff wars. BSNL's sales and distribution capacity was strengthened and for the first time channel partners were roped in. With all these measures and more it is hoped that BSNL could also become another elephant that can dance. As Gerstner said, when the elephant begins to dance all the ants will leave the dance floor.

In the long history of humankind (and animal kind, too) those who learned to collaborate and improvise most effectively have prevailed.

— Charles Darwin

DARWIN'S ORIGIN OF SPECIES
(The Law of Natural Selection)

Evolution is through a process of natural selection wherein individuals display differences and compete for resources.
Only the fittest survive in the constant struggle for survival and existence.

'EVERY BOOK IS LIKE ANY OTHER BOOK AND UNLIKE ANY other book,' said someone. So is it with people. People are all alike yet different in their own ways. People compete with each other in different degrees and play fair or foul. What we all want are things that are valued and cherished and the resources or means to achieve them are things to be competed for. It is here that the ends and means blend seamlessly. In this twilight zone are what we call power, money, authority, love and all their assorted concomitants.

In this daily and eternal struggle, the fittest wins. The fittest is the one who adapts within to the changes out there.

The fittest does not endeavor for a total upheaval of one's attitudes, values or lifestyle. The fittest remains faithful to all that are dear to his or her heart and mind, yet he or she re-orients them in alignment with changes in the circumstances.

Of late, change management has become a fancy word in the theory of leadership. Most such theories begin with or end up in what is known as the fallacy of Petitio Principii or 'circular reasoning' in logic. They demonstrate a conclusion by means of a premise that assumes the very conclusion.

Before 'managing' change, one must understand change, its roots and its forms. Blindly ushering it or embracing it could prove to be detrimental to both the individual and the organization. The flow of change has to be natural and one must naturally flow with it rather than imposing it or being imposed by it. Paradoxically change reinforces uniqueness and originality. The essence or ethos of what 'was' continues to be in what 'is', and what 'will' be.

Success in personal and professional life does not require you to change dramatically from who you are. All you need to do is to adapt in different degrees and ways. 'Change for the sake of change' is like putting the cart before the horse. Paul Galvin, the founder of Motorola, did not change his purpose in life, but only adapted Motorola to adjust to the changes in the socio-economic milieu.

Soichiro Honda did not change his mission of contributing to rebuild a war-torn Japan. He merely adapted his motorcycle design to suit the cultural milieu of each country. When Honda entered the 'machoistic' motorcycle market of the US dominated by the burly Harley Davidson , it did not itself turn burly. A few minor changes like the shape of handle bars of the Honda Super Cub, which went on to resemble the eyebrows of the Buddha, was all that was needed.

Ray Kroc, the founder of McDonald's adapted his dishes to the culinary tastes of different segments of customers, while the burger was itself the same. Bill Gates did not create his own operating system for IBM when he got his first breakthrough. He bought over and adapted an existing one called QDOS, made a few modifications and christened it MS-DOS.

Adaptation can at times appear to be revolutionary rather than evolutionary. The process of change may appear to be a clear break with the past, as it indeed could be but very rarely. In reality, there is always continuity 'in' change too as much as there is continuity 'and' change.

The Department of Telecommunications (DoT) was turned into Bharat Sanchar Nigam Ltd (BSNL) overnight on 1 October 2000. But even after over a decade, the process of adaptation is still on. BSNL is still seeking a balance between its social commitments as a public sector organization and a full-fledged corporation facing acute competition in a liberalized telecom sector.

An analogy from biological sciences would serve well here. Morphology is the study of structural features of an organism (like the skeleton) and physiology deals with the functions of organs. In terms of change management, one could say that while the morphology is the mission and purpose of an organization's existence, physiology is its internal systems and sub-systems that function or act to achieve that purpose. The systems and organs change and evolve but the essential structure continues.

This is abundantly explicit in the theory of evolution of Hardy and Weinberg that follows.

HARDY AND WEINBERG'S CONDITIONS FOR EVOLUTION

For evolution of species to occur, there must necessarily be certain conditions such as mutation, natural selection, selective and non-random breeding, migration and difference in offspring in the population.

WHEN RADICAL CHANGE IS WITNESSED IN THE ENVIRONMENT, the process of adaptation is more pronounced. A discussion on sudden and massive upheavals that radically affect the way business is conducted finds place in the earlier part of this book. Andy Grove, the CEO of Intel, called these Strategic Inflection Points. Yet, there is almost always a continuity 'in' change. Intel itself which went through one such upheaval switched from memory chips to microprocessors. It did not jump from chips to making champagne.

After the World War II, Boeing lost a huge demand for its carrier aircraft from the military establishment. Boeing simply adapted its carriers into aerial refuelling aircraft. This met the need of long-haul flights which did not have to land in order to refuel. Instances of a caterpillar going to sleep and emerging as a rabbit are rare in the real world.

Changes to external environment do not per se cause evolution or adaptation. It is the response to external conditions that causes it.

A leader must understand that the state of being of the people (as defined in the earlier chapters) and the ethos of organizations do mutate as a part of the adaptive process. Elements of the old are retained but the new is dominant and visible.

The transformation of the self and the organization is subtle and at times shrouded in an aura of the mystic. The past melts into the new, becoming an inseparable, indistinguishable part of the present, though not easily discernible as such. At an individual level, leadership acumen consists in recognizing your *dosha* type (*vatta, pitta, kappa* (as explained in Chapter 2) and fine tuning your Dominant Energy Differentiator.

At an organizational level, natural selection takes place by a movement to new markets, by adapting new business processes and inculcation of new skill sets into existing employees. It can also be by inducting those with such skill sets who fit into the evolutionary organization's needs quite naturally.

By upgrading the knowledge levels and skill sets of the existing employees, selective inbreeding of talent is achieved within the organization. By consciously picking up and placing such persons in selective positions, differentiation is achieved between organizations. This in turn results in competitive advantage of one organization over the other and comparative advantage of one nation over another.

Even as evolution progresses in nature, new discoveries have been made that reveal startling possibilities about the world around us and the laws by which it operates. The most recent and enthralling one is the 'string theory' in physics. According to the string theory, the fundamental particles that make up matter are not really particles at all – they are actually tiny vibrating strings. String theory provides for many different types of strings. The theory postulates a fundamental unity of all that exists. All are pieces of cloth which maybe of different sizes and shapes but cut from one and the same cosmic 'fabric'. Everything changes and evolves at one level, but everything is related and kindred at another. Evolution is convergent.

A true leader is half philosopher and poet. He binds the team in a seamless unity. He leads alone, yet leads 'together'.

Om Sahanaa Vavatu Sahanau Bhunaktu
Saha Veeryam Karavaavahai
Tejasvi Naavadheetamastu Maa Vidvishaavahai
Om Shantih Shantih Shantih

— *Taittiriya Upanishad*

'Together let us live and enjoy life, together let us eat, together let us work, let us stand in support of each other together, and let us not do anything that may poison our being together.'